Voices from the Margin
A Translation of Selected Odia Short Stories

Voices from the Margin
A Translation of Selected Odia Short Stories

Translated by
Anjali Tripathy

BLACK EAGLE BOOKS
Dublin, USA | Bhubaneswar, India

 Black Eagle Books
USA address:
7464 Wisdom Lane
Dublin, OH 43016

India address:
E/312, Trident Galaxy, Kalinga Nagar,
Bhubaneswar-751003, Odisha, India

E-mail: info@blackeaglebooks.org
Website: www.blackeaglebooks.org

First International Edition Published by
Black Eagle Books, 2024

VOICES FROM THE MARGIN
(A Translation of Selected Odia Short Stories)
by **Eminent Authors**

Translated by **Anjali Tripathy**

Translation Copyright © Anjali Tripathy

All rights reserved. No part of this publication may be reproduced, stored in a retrieval system, or transmitted, in any form or by any means, electronic, mechanical, photocopying, recording or otherwise without the prior permission of the publisher.

Cover & Interior Design: Ezy's Publication

ISBN- 978-1-64560-283-5 (Paperback)
Library of Congress Control Number: 2024941062

Printed in the United States of America

Contents

Preface	7
Acknowledgement	15
Abani Kumar Baral's "The Bamboo Queen"	17
Bhagabati Charan Panigrahi's "Jungli"	24
Durga Madhab Mishra's "Buda Kirisani"	31
Pranabandhu Kar's "The Vanquished"	38
Pranabandhu Kar's "Two Friends"	45
Rajat Mohapatra's "The Daughter of Niyamagiri"	54
Bhubaneswar Behera's "The Flying Fringe"	61
Gayatri Saraf's "The Burning Mountain"	75
Tarunakanti Mishra's "Rebati"	86
Kamalakanta Das' "The Allure of Ghasi Lane"	97
Glossary	109
Bio-notes of Authors	112

Preface

The stories selected for this anthology of translation include contemporary tales drawn from various authors and cover a variety of themes. The opening story Abani Kumar Baral's "The Bamboo Queen" ("Baunsa Rani" in Odia) presents the predicament of the community of nomads, especially the women, who live on showing acrobatics on the bamboo. A previous version of my translation of the story was published in the journal *Sanglap* (July 2023) with the editorial comments of Samrat Sengupta, the editor-in-chief of the journal. Sengupta remarks,

The story deals with the complex question of caste, class, gender, and the crisis of subaltern women belonging to the community of nomadic acrobats, performing feats on the streets and roaming from place to place. The women playing on bamboo sticks and swinging freely above the ground, as represented in the story, suggest the ambiguous spatial relationship they share with mainstream society and their precarious existence. The game is supposedly a surviving trace of performative cultures that predates literacy and connects with other nomadic communities of the world, like the gypsies who roam from place to place and lack a permanent foothold in the mainstream sedentary society. The homelessness of this community in the story takes a more complex turn when we see the predicament of women from this community.

The included tales in the volume draw their characters primarily from the margins of the society – the tribals, nomads, women and children. Bhagabati Charan Panigrahi's "Jungli," Durga Madhab Mishra's "Buda Kirisani," Pranabandhu Kar's "The Vanquished" and "Two Friends," Rajat Mohapatra's "The Daughter of Niyamagiri" are tribal tales from Odisha.

Bhagabati Charan Panigrahi's "Jungli" ("Jungli" in Odia original) unfolds a tale both enchanting and tragic, wherein a solitary man lives amidst the untamed wilderness. His existence, nestled within a cavern deep within the jungle's embrace, is forever altered by the unexpected arrival of a *shabar* maiden, herself lost amidst the labyrinthine foliage. Their relation, a brief interlude, is severed with the arrival of the maiden's father, who takes her away. The narrative, at its heart, is a poignant exploration of love and loss. It mourns the fleeting beauty of their connection. Jungli's demise, met at the hands of the maiden's father who tore them asunder, stands as a somber testament to the cruelty of fate. The tale also poses the stark dichotomy between the innocent affection of the woodland creatures and the possessive grasp of humanity, each vying for dominance within the tangled undergrowth of the jungle's heart.

The next story in the collection, Durga Madhab Mishra's "Buda Kirisani" (titled "Buda Kirisani" in Odia original), named after its protagonist, unfolds the significance of the Chaitra festival in the life of Buda Kirisani. It recounts the day when Buda Kirisani, amidst the festivities, encountered and pledged eternal companionship to Lachchami, only to lose her after fourteen years, on that very same day. Embedded within the narrative are profound insights into the customs and traditions of Kirisani's tribal community, offering a glimpse into their way of life. In Pranabandhu Kar's poignant narrative, "The Vanquished" ("Parahata" in Odia), one is drawn towards the clandestine rebellion of Sunti, a *paana* Christian woman, against the perceived superiority of the aristocracy. Her bold articulation of desire and her overt invitation to an unknown traveler, ultimately revealing its deeper significance, serves as a poignant commentary on the complexities of civilized society. Sunti candidly unveils the paradox of her existence – while many are drawn to her allure, none are willing to accept her as a spouse. The affluent gentlemen clandestinely revel in her captivating presence, indulging in embraces shrouded in secrecy. Yet, Sunti finds a perverse satisfaction in observing the contortions of their muscles, the intensity of their gaze, juxtaposed with their profound vulnerability and powerlessness in her presence. In another of Kar's tribal tales, "Two Friends," the readers are tenderly ushered into the lives of Basali and Mudani, two young *kondh* women who navigate the tumult of love and loss as their men are claimed by the ravages of war.

In Rajat Mohapatra's evocative tale, "The Daughter of Niyamagiri" ("Niyamagiri ra Jhia" in Odia), the stage is set amidst the rugged expanse of Niyamagiri, a majestic hill range nestled in the districts of Kalahandi and Rayagada in the southwest of Odisha, India. Within these ancient peaks resides the indigenous *dangaria kondh*, their lives intricately woven into the fabric of this untamed terrain. The heart of these hills cradles one of India's last bastions of pristine wilderness, a sanctuary of verdant splendor teeming with life. Niyamagiri emerged into the spotlight when the impacts of a decision by the Environment and Forest Ministry of the Government of India echoed across the land. This decision, to rescind a forest clearance granted to the mining conglomerate Vedanta Resources, reverberated with profound implications. The cancellation of the mining project marked a victory for the *dangaria kondh* and *kutia kondh* tribes, classified as "Primitive Tribal Groups," for whom these verdant slopes and meandering streams serve as the very pulse of existence, warranting special protection. The Niyamagiri massif stands as a bastion of biodiversity, its sprawling canopy bridging a tapestry of forests and wildlife sanctuaries. Revered by the two *kondh* communities as sacred ground, the hills are not merely a habitat but a lifeline, upon which their survival hinges. In a momentous turn of events in 2013, the highest court of India deferred to the wisdom of the tribal people, who resoundingly rejected the proposed project in the hallowed halls of their village councils, reaffirming their stewardship of the land and its delicate ecosystem.

In Mohapatra's narrative, the eldest *dangaria kondh*, revered as the Niyama King among the indigenous denizens of the Niyamagiri region, stands as a guardian of time-honored principles. Under his benevolent rule, a code of conduct is upheld, where hunger and nakedness are banished from the realm, and the sanctity of nature is fiercely protected. Within this verdant kingdom, the forest bestows its bounty upon its inhabitants, and the earth itself is deemed sacred, forbidden from being bartered away. In the kingdom of the Niyama King, the allure of city life is shunned, its trappings of deception viewed as a veil obscuring truth. The bonds of trust between kinfolk are sacrosanct, betrayal deemed a harbinger of encroaching urbanity, its sweet deceit corroding the fabric of tribal unity. Amidst this idyllic tableau, the fate of Jhumki, a *dangaria kondh* orphan girl sheltered under the Niyama King's protective wing, takes a tragic turn. Ensnared by the influence of the outsider, Bideshi, her demise by drowning serves as a tender testament to the encroaching tendrils of civilization, heralding the unraveling of tribal traditions and the inexorable march of destruction upon their ancient way of life.

In Bhubaneswar Behera's "The Flying Fringe" ("Phara Phara Ude Panata Kani" in Odia), the readers are drawn into a narrative that delves deep into the intricate web of human relationships, where innocence meets exploitation in the heart of a tribal community. As the story unfolds, one gets a glimpse into the humble existence of Tulu and his wife Bhainri, both deeply entrenched in the traditions and customs of their *shabar* community. In their village life, simplicity reigns supreme and the bonds of trust are held sacred. Yet, lurking beneath the surface lies the ever-present threat of exploitation. In the story, Tulu's simplicity and unquestioning trust stand in stark contrast to the cunning machinations employed by the *sahukar* to exploit Tulu's naivety for personal gain.

In the collection, Gayatri Saraf's story "The Burning Mountain" stands as a resolute anthem for feminism. Within its pages unfolds the tale of Ukia and her husband, Samara, seekers of elusive dreams in a distant land, drawn to toil in the unforgiving crucible of a brick kiln in pursuit of a brighter horizon. Yet, their aspirations are cruelly dashed as Ukia becomes ensnared in the master's web of sexual exploitation, while Samara meets his tragic end in a futile bid to resist. Retreating to her village with their daughter, Ukia finds solace elusive, her existence shrouded in the darkness that belies her very name, for Ukia, in its essence, signifies light. The narrative's inception finds her beseeching Sarojini, a writer hailing from the privileged echelons of urban society, to immortalize her plight in the annals of literature. Through the prism of Ukia's harrowing journey, Saraf casts a searing spotlight on the scourges of poverty, rural dislocation, the brutal exploitation of female laborers, and the sinister specter of trafficking, underscoring a litany of interconnected social maladies.

This potent narrative has transcended linguistic barriers, finding resonance in Supriya Kar's anthology *Burning Mountains*, where it has been translated and enshrined alongside a constellation of other luminous Odia tales. Seemita Mohanty, in her anthology *Different Women, Different Worlds: Ten Short Stories by Odia Women Writers*, similarly includes Saraf's work, originally titled "Jali Jali Jauthiba Pahada" in Odia, retitling it "The Mountain That Burns" in a testament to the enduring vitality of literary translation, where each rendition breathes new life into the original narrative tapestry without forfeiting its inherent essence.

Similarly, Fakir Mohan Senapati's timeless tale "Rebati" has been subjected to multiple adaptations crafted by various pens. In Tarunakanti Mishra's rendition of "Rebati," a heart-wrenching narrative unfolds – a father, driven by desperation or perhaps coercion, consigns his tender daughter, not yet sixteen, into the clutches of a Kolkata brothel. The motives behind the father's actions remain shrouded in ambiguity, yet the cruel hand of fate spares no mercy for the innocent girl.

"The Allure of Ghasi Lane" ("Ghasi Pada ra Maya" in Odia) by Kamalakanta Das tells the story of Minaketan who is transferred to a place. He and his brahmin family choose to stay in quarters close to the *ganda* and *ghasi* lanes inhabited by people who are considered untouchables. Amidst the humble abodes of lower castes, they forge bonds, kindling flames of empathy and understanding. A symphony of camaraderie ensues, as they extend hands of assistance and ignite sparks of societal change. He is prepared to risk his job for their love. Through its narrative weave, the story echoes a poignant sermon on the sanctity of human connection, a defiant rebuttal against the shackles of discrimination and prejudice.

I must mention that in the pursuit of translating these narratives, the endeavor extends beyond mere replication of plot and character. It is an odyssey to encapsulate the very essence, the raw emotions that pulsate within the original tales. This effort demands a delicate equilibrium between the literal and the metaphorical, a skillful attempt to capture the rhythm of language and preserve the cultural nuances that imbue the story with its profound significance. The translator does not lay claim to absolute fidelity to the source text, for within the realm of literary translation, the notion of faithfulness is but a fleeting illusion. Meanings metamorphose, adapting to the gaze of the translator as the interpreter, each rendition a pilgrimage into a new cultural realm rather than a mere linguistic transmutation. In this realm, fidelity yields to interpretation, as translation emerges as a deeply subjective and interpretative art form, where accommodation and adaptation are inevitable companions on the journey.

Acknowledgement

The stories included in the collection have been sourced from various anthologies of Odia short stories. Abani Kumar Baral's "The Bamboo Queen", Durga Madhab Mishra's "Buda Kirisani", Pranabandhu Kar's "The Vanquished" and Kamalakanta Das' "The Allure of Ghasi Lane" have been selected from *Shreshtha Odia Galpa Sankalana* compiled by Mahapatra Nilamani Sahoo published by Odisha Sahitya Academy in 1985. Pranabandhu Kar's "Two Friends" is sourced from *Pranabandhu Kar Granthabali* published by Vidyapuri, Cuttack, 1998. Bhagabati Charan Panigrahi's "Jungli" is borrowed from *Bhagabati Sanchayana* published by Nabajuga Granthalaya, Cuttack in 1985. Rajat Mohapatra's "The Daughter of Niyamagiri" is taken from *Swadhinottara Odia Khyudra Galpa* published by Sahitya Academy. Bhubaneswar Behera's "The Flying Fringe" is extracted from *Bhubaneswar Behera Sahitya Samagra* compiled and edited by Yashodhara Mishra and published by Ink Odisha, Bhubaneswar in 2012. Gayatri Saraf's "The Burning Mountain" is included from *Odia Galpa Samhara* compiled and edited by Jatindra Mohan Mohanty published by Vidya, Bhubaneswar in 2006. Tarunakanti Mishra's "Rebati" is extracted from the author's collection *Bitansa* (Friends publishers).

The Bamboo Queen

Abani Kumar Baral

"Is the game over daughter?"
"Yes, papa."
"How much is left?"
"Much of it."

The sound of *dhol* (drum) can be heard. Labanga climbs the smooth, yellow, and straight bamboo like a monkey, following the beat. On top of it, she sits with swinging legs, singing as if she is the daughter of the sky – the bamboo queen Labanga. Sita, her younger sister, rises to the same beat as her. She sits on the opposite side.

Then both the sisters start swinging on the rope. Labanga remains in the swinging position. Her younger sister stands balancing her legs and shoulders keeping her hands suspended in the air. The watching eyes widen in wonder, the heads of the onlookers whirl and the flower from the *brahmin*'s ear falls, while beholding the scene. The village street resounds with applaud. Sita comes down. Now on the disk on the bamboo Labanga lies with her face, heavy breast and legs down and moves round and round with great speed. Her plaits open and look like two thin bamboo sticks. She keeps moving without taking support of her hands and legs. She could view people coming below and giving money, uncooked rice (carried in their dirty clothes) and full bowls of cooked rice in appreciation of her performance.

Labanga and her family keep moving from village to village and street to street with all their belongings – rice and dals of all types mixed together, oil, salt and pot – everything. Today they are here and tomorrow they will be elsewhere. The drum beats in the show of the bamboo queen. People listen to its sound and assemble; the bamboo rises to the sky and with it rises the bamboo queen Labanga.

Labanga is the middle daughter of Mania Kela; Jhampa is the eldest daughter and Sita is the youngest. They live in tents in mango groves, under big trees or verandas of small schools. Mania sets out in the morning with Sita, Labanga and Jhampa and the drum beater young man Dinua to show the game to earn his livelihood. The old woman is left behind to cook.

Labanga is a strong girl. She may be twenty-two or twenty-three. Her dark body has pillar like thighs. She wears thick eye-liner in the eyes, black dot on the forehead. Wearing a tight blouse makes it convenient for her to show the game. She laughs a hearty laugh when people joke at her. She throws her saree and climbs the smooth straight bamboo. Like the circus girls, she wears tight pants inside to cover her thighs. The greedy eyes of the hunters make a survey of her strong "desirable" body just like the tiger approaching its prey. Knowingly, she blinks her eye at some inciting their desire. Some people wait in expectation. Standing on the high rope, Labanga starts singing loud, "Yesterday I went to bring water…" She looks at Dinua, smiles and sings again.

Now it is Sita's turn. She will complete thirteen soon

and the bony places of her chest are turning fleshy. Shyly, she also opens her cloth. The hungry eyes around her close and then open. She is wearing silk pants and a blouse. Perhaps, someone has gifted. Sita climbs the bamboo and the game continues. Staying on the ground Jhampa shows performance of different types. She may be thirty or thirty-five. She has started developing rough features. In spite of having *kajol* in eyes, a bun of oiled black hair and high breasts, she looks wild. Softness of features has abandoned her.

With self-satisfaction old Mania glances at his daughters once, then at the scattered money on the *gamcha* (towel). He wipes his moustache and starts showing tricks with iron balls. Earlier, he used to beat the drum. Dinua joined them before two or two and a half years. It was perhaps in 1973. He doesn't know the name of the village. Mania had gone for a show with his troop. Orphan, unsheltered Dinua came to him. Dinua had roamed around many towns and had worked at several places. He had even worked in a band party and knew how to play drum, trumpet, *mahuri*, and many other musical instruments. Nobody in that village knew about his caste or family; people called him Dinu, Dilu, Dilbar, etc. Some thought him a Muslim; others assumed him an outcaste.

Dinua had come to watch the game. Labanga gave him a coquettish glance. Dinua returned the look. After that, Labanga had wanted to look at him again and again. But Dinua could not look at her eyes. Routinely, Labanga smilingly came close to people to ask for money after the performance. But she could not raise her eyes, when she stood near Dinua. Dinua gave all the money he had in Labanga's hand that day.

"Do you want to starve baboo?"

Dinua replied with a smile only.

In the evening a well-dressed young man came to Mania and pleaded him, "Sardar! Will you take me with you? I can play drum and many other instruments. I will follow you wherever you go."

The bamboo king Mania had never dreamt of keeping another person to assist him in playing the drum, but he agreed. "I don't have any money," he said.

Dinua said, "I don't need money. I will eat with you. Give me some pocket money only. If you had a son, won't he do it?"

Mania thought of his three daughters and wife. How long could he continue like this? At this ripe age, it would be a great support to have a man with him. From that day, wearing a lungi with a *dhol* on his shoulders, Dinua has been wandering with them from village to village, from town to town. Every evening sleeping in the shade of the tree playing a flute, he waits for the call of the old woman to eat his meal. On some nights the old woman says, "We will break the group and get the girls married." They have been thinking like this since long and in the meantime, Jhampa has become thirty-five, Labanga has grown, Sita is growing. No, they will not be given in marriage. Mania often says, "Let them go wherever they want to after I die. I have nothing to say." Mania once heard Jhampa and Labanga talking, "How long shall we provide for our old parents by showing our bodies? We get more money for wearing tight pants and blouse than for the performance on the rope." Initially, Jhampa tried to forbid Labanga to do that, "Why don't you cover your body with that cloth?" Mania sharply said, "Why? Will people swallow you?" Now they don't feel ashamed. Exhibiting the body is a routine of Labanga; winking the eyes is her profession.

Her father has taught her this. When people lay hands on her cheek or back or press her hands, she does not react. Jhampa *apa* (elder sister) has told her that people did that to her also. The same thing will happen to Sita. Her father has taught her to take it easy.

"Nobody comes to see our performance. They come to see our body." Jhampa has told her. Labanga has seen Jhampa crying at times in the night. Jagua, whom they met at Manpur, was chasing her. Jhampa was laughing with him and was happy in his company. Labanga has seen them embracing each other tightly in the groves an evening. Jagua was kissing Jhampa and she was looking at him happily. She doesn't know what happened after that, but one day father beat Jhampa. Jagua stopped seeing her. Mania waited for him with a sharp axe. He no longer comes in secret also. Dinua may meet the same end. But Mania likes him very much. Labanga understands it all, but pretends ignorance. She muses on Jhampa *apa*'s mistakes, but fails to find any. Only she wanted to tightly hug Jagua and become one with him. What is the mistake?

Labanga thought, "Why should I earn money by showing my body? If I run away, this show business will slow down. Sita has to act like her for next four or five years. Her elder sister can't do it anymore. Her body has lost the charm. People no longer pay attention to her and leave when she performs on the bamboo. She has seen her wiping tears in secret.

It's evening now. The last flicker of fire is lurking beneath the ash in the oven. Mania goes to sleep. On the other side of the grove, in the shade of a tree Dinua rests his head on a bundle of clothes and softly plays the flute. With stealthy steps, Labanga approaches towards him, puts her head on his laps and starts narrating endless tales. Dinua overloads her with kisses, but Labanga never gives herself away.

Now, Labanga does not enjoy the jokes of the audience during her performance. She thinks, will she live her whole life by showing her body to others in this way? How long will she play with fire and remain away from it? The fire is burning her. She wishes to become ash. The other day Jhampa advised her, "Labanga, go with Dinua to a far off place. You will be happy, even if you starve. Also, Dinua can play the drum and you play the bamboo queen to earn your livelihood. Go soon; else you will have my fate. When you grow older, nobody will look at you. So, go wherever your eyes direct." Labanga could not sleep the whole night thinking of it. An unknown excitement grips her. Lost in a tender beautiful dream world, she smiles and laughs unconsciously. The peaceful mango groves, the shady sky have transported her into a world where she finds only Dinua and there is no sign of her father. Dinua is walking in the front with *dhol* on his shoulders and bamboo in his hand and she is following him carrying other things in a bundle of cloth. After that…sleep…night…happy life.

With her head on Dinua's chest, Labanga ponders, how to relate him her mind. How will she persuade him to elope with her? Dinua plays another tune while caressing her head. Labanga asks, "How was the show today?"

"Good."

"You liked it. Isn't it?"

"I don't like watching the same act every day. I watch only because you play."

After each short interchange, Labanga is thinking how to propose. Will she elope with this outsider, leaving behind the wet eyes of Sita, Jhampa, father, and mother? The confusion and hesitation in her mind start mounting.

It is already dark. The gekkering of the foxes is heard from a distance. On the village road a few people are seen returning home.

Suddenly, she finds Dinua unfamiliar. Labanga thinks, like all others, he looks at her with fondness and winks his eyes. Why will he take her burden? He is no different from others. Tonight will pass. The darkness is thickening in the mango groves. Labanga feels that she is sleeping on the chest of a ghost. There is no beating of the heart. She is clinging to a corpse. After all, she is the bamboo queen. She cannot belong to one person.

From a distance is heard Mania's voice…Labanga… Dinua…

Labanga leaves Dinua and starts running. Dinua is staring at the invisible road. He has to tell a lot of things to the bamboo queen and he wants to listen to her response. But from the dark groves, only a sliding sound emerges, and the night releases an agonising sigh.

❑

Note:
- "Baunsa Rani" means "The Bamboo Queen" which is an old Indian art form in which young girls walk on tight ropes barefoot. They also often perform a variety of acrobatic positions on the rope. This dance style is extremely risky and demands extensive training.

Jungli

Bhagabati Charan Panigrahi

He's beyond creation; he seemed to be a man from his form, but there was no trace of maleness in him. He had no religion, no caste, no society – it seemed he himself was a national animal. He looked like a man, but his nature was entirely different from that of humans. His big black body looked terrible. Except for the small triangle covering the forehead, two eyes, and the nose, all other parts of the head were covered with dense black hair and beard in such a way that the lips were not visible and the two ears could barely be seen. His whole body was covered with long black hair. He had the strength of a demon. He seemed to be an incarnation of prehistoric man in this age.

He lived inside a cave amidst dense forest. It is doubtful whether man had ever visited that place before him. It was beyond one's imagination how a human child came to that place. Perhaps just as an insect is created inside a rotten fruit, even in the absence of parents, his life was created out of the chasm of terrible darkness, as if the terrible darkness of the whole earth had condensed to express itself in the shape of this man.

He had a strange sense of beauty. If he saw a flower blooming, he would subtract the petals one by one. If the cuckoo sang, he would answer with a harsh voice. If the South wind excited him, he would devastate the whole jungle in utter madness. He started a war against the elephant, the lion, the tiger, or any other animal, he came across. In the dark stormy night of the rainy season, he would think of a honeymoon with the lioness.

He had acquaintance with the animals in the forest. Sometimes he played with them, sometimes he quarrelled with them, and brought about a war. During such fights, he was no less terrible than an animal. Sometimes he climbed the tree, abruptly attacked the opponents, and hid himself behind a tree. He attacked so many in a flicker of the eyes that it was impossible to imagine that he was human. He had been injured many times during such fights; he recovered and fought again.

He had acquaintance with many inhabitants of the jungle, but his relation with the deer was of much interest. The deer was fickle and playful. She would jump from this end to that end of the jungle in a moment, would play with other deer. She could not resist soft grass; the slow breeze would excite her, and she would raise her head to look around as if she were smelling its fragrance. She would dance happily. The *jungli* was glad to witness all these, but sometimes he was angry with the deer for her playful nature. When the deer ran, he followed, but he could not match her speed. The deer left him far behind. She did not wait for him. When the deer left him, though he wanted to be near her, he became angry. He promised to himself to attack her, when she returned. But when the deer softly touched his hairy cheek, he forgot anger and embraced her. The deer had developed affection for this terrible animal.

She played, wandered, and grazed with the deer, but she was not that intimate with anyone. When she sensed or apprehended any danger, she took refuge in her human friend. When the deer was injured, the friend cared and nursed. When the friend is injured by the lion or the tiger, the deer took care to lessen his pain. They spent their days in this manner.

II

One day, a *shabar* girl in her sweet sixteen forgot her path in the dark night and reached the cave. The faint light of dawn had already started lighting the surroundings at that time. The tired maiden sat on a stone in front of the cave. The forest-dwelling man had awakened and started playing endearingly with the deer. He was not conscious of the outside surroundings; he was playing inside the cave. Suddenly, he glanced at the surroundings and saw a maiden sitting. The maiden's face looked beautiful, lit by the golden light of the sun, though her eyes seemed anxious in apprehension. Jungli was astonished to witness such an amazing creation. After some time, he came out of the cave, slowly approached the girl, and hugged her.

The maiden was in deep thought; she startled at the sudden touch. When she saw the giant naked statue of a man in front of her, she shrieked and fell unconscious. Jungli was shocked at the shriek and could not comprehend its meaning. He thought for some time and started slowly caressing her. The maiden came to her senses and saw that the man did not intend to harm her. She calmed down and abandoned her fear.

The *shabar* maiden saw that it was impossible for her to find her way in the dense forest. She had to take shelter in the jungle's place. Tears rolled down her eyes continuously when she remembered her home – her father, mother, brother, and sister. But Jungli did not find any reason for these tears. He caressed her, he wiped her tears, but such affection only aggravated her cry. Jungli looked at her with large, uncomprehending eyes.

Jungli was ecstatic to find the maiden; his life became happier. Sometimes he embraced the maiden and sometimes the deer. Sometimes he danced in front of both of them. He brought a variety of fruits from the jungle for the maiden to appease her. He performed a lot of playful acts with the deer to please her.

Within a few days, Jungli became surprised to observe the activities of the *shabar* maiden. This young woman could make utensils of mud, make fire by rubbing two polished stones, and prepare meat and vegetable dishes in the mud utensils by making use of fire. She did not climb the tree, still got the fruit by using a long bamboo stick. She kept the living space clean and in order. These were not small things for Jungli. He pondered that she belonged to a higher class of animals, and she had some distinct qualities. He felt intimidated in front of her. He bestowed respect and restraint.

The maiden took advantage of his weakness and showed mastery over him. She went on ordering him to do different works, and Jungli was always ready to carry out the orders. The maiden taught him language and rendered him advice to comfortably complete various works. Jungli had changed a lot due to her. He had gradually abandoned his animal nature. He could speak a little. He no longer fought with the animals.

One could not presume with certainty whether the *shabar* girl loved Jungli. When she saw that the man had intimate relations with the deer, she grew envious. She started misbehaving with her. Sometimes she drove her out of the house by beating, and sometimes she kicked her. When the deer looked at Jungli with empathy, the maiden laughed loud and like a machine, Jungli echoed that laughter. The deer left the place in silence, but Jungli failed to notice. He was enchanted by the maiden. Sometimes he also drove the deer into the cave and joined the laughter of the maiden.

One day, the maiden wished to kill and cook the deer. Till then, the young man had carried out all the orders and requests of the maiden. But he could not carry out this order. He killed another deer and gave it to the woman. After that, the jealousy and anger of the woman towards the deer doubled. She started torturing the deer more cruelly. The deer helplessly tolerated all her misbehavior, still she did not leave the cave. What expectation she had from the Jungli, one could not state. Now Jungli could not hug the maiden anytime he wanted. He was scared. When he went to embrace her, he returned with a lowered head due to the cold response of the maiden. His courage failed there. When the maiden understood that the man was hurt, she smilingly ordered him to do something. Jungli forgot everything by looking at her smiling face. He hurried to do the work. The maiden laughed in heart to see this.

III

One day, suddenly the maiden saw her father crossing the pathway. At that time, Jungli was not in the cave. The maiden excitedly called her father. The father recognized the voice of the daughter and looked back. The maiden rushed to the father. The father embraced the daughter and asked, "Where were you for so long?" The daughter pointed at the cave. The father was surprised to think how did she stay alone in the terrible place. Then he narrated the history of the cave. He told her that a bandit inhabited the cave twenty years ago. That bandit had a baby boy of two or three years old. One day he had gone to rob, leaving the child in the cave. He was caught and sent to lifetime imprisonment. Nobody knew what happened to his son after that. The maiden could understand that Jungli was his son, but she did not dare to tell her father about the man. She was worried about "what would her father say," if he knew that she was staying with the Jungli.

The father set out with the daughter. The *shabar* maiden was excited to go home. At the same time, she was hesitant to leave the innocent Jungli forever. She wanted to take Jungli with her, but how could she convey it to her father? She kept it to herself. They had taken only a few steps forward, when a terrible sound reached their ears from behind. A stone hit the maiden's father. He saw that a terrible man was rushing towards them with a branch of a tree in his hand. He could not find any other way and set the target with his arrow. The maiden trembled and wanted to stop her father, but before she could utter anything, the arrow pierced the giant hairy body of Jungli. He shrieked and fell. The maiden sought refuge on her father's shoulder. The *shabar* thought that his daughter was horrified at the sight, and he left the place hurriedly with her.

Blood flowed from the broad chest of Jungli. His untamed body trembled for some time and then became still forever. The silent deer was washing the wound with her tears.

❑

Note:
- Jungli, in its literal sense, denotes dwelling in an Indian forest or possessing the qualities of one who inhabits

such a setting. The protagonist bears the name Jungli as a reflection of his upbringing amidst wilderness, devoid of human companionship, and symbolizing a state of being wild and untamed.

Buda Kirisani

Durga Madhab Mishra

He is thinking.
Buda Kirisani.
Half-burnt cigarette in ear, cone of *siali* leaf in mouth – when sucked in the dark, it emits red fire.
Someone is beating the drum at a distance and the sound of *dung-dunga* is overheard.
Chaita Parab (Chaitra festival).
"Oh! Today is *Chaita Parab*."
After the Chaitra festival of that day, fourteen other Chaitra festival have passed in Buda Kirisani's life like the blink of an eye. Somebody has engraved the Chaitra festival of that day on his bony frame. Every Chaitra festival freezes that frame and emanates a few drops of blood from his body.
When the young Buda Kirisani was not married, he had the strength of an elephant. Nobody could match his strength in the entire forest area. He used to pace from Khairaput to Pindajungar village and come back without resting anywhere – a distance of seventeen miles – as if he was going to the nearby pond for a call of nature.
Buda Kirisani laughs. He looks at his weak bony wrinkled chest and laughs in his sadness. Oh! How loudly the drum beats and the *dung-dunga* perfectly matches

the beat. Whatever blood remains in his body multiplies fourfold. In his white haired body, there is madness for burnt cultivation. In front of his house the fire lurks beneath the ashes. He doesn't have the strength to take out the ashes. Who is there? Who is there with him? True, he has nobody now.

Buda Kirisani takes a deep breath.

"Oh! It's unbearable. Life has become useless."

He coughs. Fresh red blood comes out.

"If Lachchami (tribal form of Lakshmi) were there today...," he thinks. Like a torn rope, the veins in his neck release water droplets and they run to the corner of his eyes. He tries to suck the smoke – but meanwhile it extinguishes.

This happened fourteen years ago. Pindajungar to Khairaput is a distance of seventeen miles. He had taken Dangar Jamanu's carriage to Khairaput. It was already twilight when he returned. He wore a dazzling coin on his ear – his payment for bringing it so far. Buda Kirisani would return that day. That day was Chaitra festival.

The Pinda forest on the mountain would resound with laughter. And the four hand red cloth of the women would slip off with their stomach-aching laughter when they danced to the beat.

How could he stay in Khairaput on this big festival day?

Impossible.

In his absence Soma would play the *dung-dunga*. Did he even know playing anything? Buda Kirisani would have to teach him for seventeen years. He had no strength in his body. He became breathless like a pregnant woman after playing the instrument for one hour only.

Buda was walking. The close association of trees had created darkness ahead of him. Forest and darkness blended together as if a student of class three had painted black and blue in patches. Buda Kirisani didn't notice that. If he didn't reach Pindajungar, would he be called a man? He would go – Surely go.

"Oh mother! Oh mother! *Baria . . . baria...baria.*"

"What happened?"

Somebody breathlessly came and embraced Buda's body.

Darkness was enhancing.

Buda could not see clearly.

"Who is that?"

"I ... *baria.........baria.....*Ah...Ah....."

"Who are you?"

Something dark rushed from the bushes.

"Ah...Ah......Ah...."

Someone was shrieking and tightly embracing Buda. Buda's muscles tightened and his blood boiled in excitement.

"Oh, it's too dark!"

From his right arm he took his bow and an arrow from his back and took aim in the blink of an eye. The arrow hurried towards the dark animal amidst darkness. He could not go further.

Then Buda burnt a stick and started walking further. He was sweating profusely.

The arrow had hit the target. How big were the teeth of that animal? It could have ground four men in a moment. Buda pulled the arrow which had pierced the neck of the animal. Warm blood gushed like a stream.

Buda looked at his back.

Who was this?

Lachchami, Lachchami.

Bead necklaces were hanging from her neck

through her cleavage. Red, blue, yellow – there were necklaces of all colours. To both sides lie her breasts – strong and well developed. One and a half hand span red cloth covered her waist. Youth was overflowing from her every limb.

Buda made her stand with both the arms. A pitcher of water was lying nearby. He brought water with the folds of his hands and sprinkled on Lachchami's face. He wetted his *gamcha* and wiped her eyes and nose with it. He blew air into her ears. Lachchami opened her eyes.

"Oh....baria....baria..."

She fainted again. Once more he sprinkled water and she gained consciousness. She rose and tightly hugged Buda. Buda lifted her face. The flow of blood from the body of the animal had not ceased.

Baria was dead.

There was wave of blood on Lachchami's lips and gratitude and shame in her eyes.

"Where have you been *dhangri*, young woman?"

"I had gone to fill water."

"Why did you go alone?"

What would Lachchami say? The danger was already over. She smiled slowly and softly.

Buda Kirisani wiped the sweat of his strong arms and looked at Lachchami for a moment. He asked, "I will go to Pindajungar. Will you go with me woman?"

Lachchami felt lightning striking her body. Her face brimmed with redness. Lachchami knew the reason behind the question. This question comes in the life of a tribal young woman once and the tribal man wants a direct answer then and there. There is no scope for answers like "I will think and tell," "I will tell after two days," or "I will ask my father and tell." The man does not listen to such answers and goes his own way. Many young women come in the way of a man. He does not pine for one. The tribal woman knows it and knows it well.

She looked at Buda Kirisani a full moment. Buda Kirisani – he had shining full cheeks and unspoken sparkle in his eyes. He was wearing aluminium bangles on arms, traditional necklace, *gamcha* on head with a tin frame, shining white plastic belt bought from Dumuriput market on his waist, red *koupin*, bamboo-bow on right shoulder, iron-edged arrows on the back.

Warm blood was still flowing from *baria*'s body. Lachchami rushed into Buda's arms. Her youth and beauty melted before Buda's body. The branch of Pulang was burning more furiously. Buda Kirisani held Lachchami – his Lachchami – in his hands. What's this? Buda was crying. Tear streamed from his eyes and all the impurities of the eyes flew with it.

Mahuri was heard more loudly. The sounds of *dhol* and *dung-dunga* deafened the ears. The night was coming to an end. The young women of the village had become tired by continuous dancing. The moon had faded behind the hills of Pindajungar. Everyone looked tired – the effect of wine was almost over.

The *Mahuria* blew the *mahuri*. Everyone turned to look at Buda and Lachchami. All the young men and women crowded around them in excitement like flood in Giri river. Everybody understood that Buda Kirisani had brought a *dangri* (young woman) from Khairaput. Selli was warming the *dhol* near the fire. He started beating it. Buda snatched the *dung-dunga* from Somasisa's hands and started playing. He extended the fan made of peacock's feathers to Lachchami's hand. How could one forget the way Lachchami danced with that fan in hand that day? She was singing and with it overflowed her intense desire, the flood of youth.

Country liquor was cooked. Chicken was arranged and pig was brought from the lane. Goddess Mahuli looked red with sacrificial blood. The Goddess smiled.

***

Baba

Buda Kirisani looks around. Oh! Perhaps Lachchami is calling. Lachchami is the four years old daughter of Buda. With walking stick in hand, he enters the house and feeds Lachchami with rice water and makes her sleep. After drinking the remaining rice water, Buda goes out.

He remembers the Chaitra festival of the last year. All other people from his village had accompanied him. He had to kill an animal. Then only Chaitra festival would come to an end. Buda went away. Lachchami had fed rice water to her daughter and made her sleep. Then she had gone to collect the leaves. She was pregnant by seven months. After climbing the steep hills of Balidangar, Lachchami felt terribly thirsty. She reached the stream and drank water to her heart's content. She fanned herself with a leaf. Oh! How painful. She felt as if somebody was taking everything away from her.

"Issssh...."

There was smell of rotten rice water in the forest. Lachchami sensed something ominous. She looked at either side, held her stomach with both hands, and then moved forward. She had hardly walked two steps...

"Oh mother."

A tiger jumped from the other side of the mountain. It took Lachchami and went to the top of the hill in a moment. The still forest trembled with the uproar of birds. Lachchami fainted. Ah! If only Buda were there.

"Hay! Jump down, jump down."

"Where?"

All the villagers had chased the tiger for two miles. The mountain ended there. The tiger would be caught.

"Buda, the tiger has taken your wife."

It was a hill with a height of two hundred feet on both sides and the river valley dividing it in the middle. Buda saw that the top of the mountain was at a distance of fifty feet. The tiger was sitting on that top with Lachchami. How will Buda Kirisani reach there? By the time he would cross the distance, Lachchami would be no more. The tiger was playing with the body of Lachchami. Buda felt an unspeakable pain in his chest.

"Lachchami… Lachchami….Oh Lachchami…."

The forest trembled. Perhaps, Lachchami opened her eyes – those two black and scared eyes. The tiger put its front legs on Lachchami's neck. At that moment Buda's arrow pierced through the neck of the tiger. Unerring arrow. The tiger fell down hundred feet from the top of the hill with a raucous sound and Lachchami fell with it. The tiger's head clashed against the rock of the river. The villagers rushed to the spot. The tiger was dead.

Buda brought water in leaf-cup from the river and sprinkled on Lachchami. The tiger's nail had torn Lachchami's neck and the veins had come out. Her heart beat could be heard faintly. Selli fanned her with Sal leaves. Buda sprinkled more water. Somasisa drove others to let the air come near her.

Lachchami looked at Buda. There was sign of devotion in those big black eyes. She closed her eyes in Buda's arms in deep contentment and never opened those again. The beating of the heart stopped for ever.

❏

The Vanquished

Pranabandhu Kar

"Oh cycle baboo! Where are you going?"

My cycle stopped. I looked back – it was a lonely track of a hilly area. She called me from behind and didn't hesitate looking shamelessly at me while laughing. I thought, "Is she mad?" Doubtfully, I got down from the bicycle and asked, "Did you call me?"

She didn't answer and continued to gaze with a static smile.

I felt humiliated. Then I looked around. Nobody was there. It was a winter noon. Hill and forest, forest and hill – everywhere. I inspected my attire, but could not trace any reason of her call or laughter.

I was pondering: When did the *malua* girls become so bold? Generally they hide in the forest, when they see baboos with coats and pants. Only one can discover their scared eyes behind the bush and they …

I beckoned her to come near, then asked her in a rough voice, "Why did you call me?"

The young woman playfully said, "Just like that."

The fact that she was not afraid of me made me feel insulted. I was angry too and observed her from toe to tip. Youth was overflowing from her body, fearless was her fluency and her well-developed breasts exhibited shamelessness. She was clad in a blouse and a white saree. I asked, "What is your village?"

"Mitingia."

"Are you a Christian?"

She nodded. Then I enquired, "*Paana* Christian?"

"Yes."

"Why did you call me?"

"Why? What happened then? Stay if you want to, else you go."

I could not decide whether I should go or stay. I continued looking at her. She smiled, gazed, turned her neck a little and said, "What are you looking at baboo? Keep your cycle behind the bushes and come with me inside the forest."

Lonely was the mountainous valley – the dark, green Sal forest was all around. There was no covert cover to the proposal, no concealment, blatant like her high busts. A woman can express her desire to an unknown traveller in such an unabashed way. It was beyond my imagination. I was stunned. What did she think of me? I looked around with fright in my eyes. Perhaps, I would not have been so terrified even when caught by a tiger.

"What are you thinking baboo?"

Startled, I turned at her.

"Are you afraid?"

"What's your name?"

"Sunti."

"Sunti?"

"Yes."

Sunti smiled – it was a beautiful smile. Sunti's face was certainly captivating. She had a long neck. Her doe eyes expressed unrepressed desire sometimes, and at times displayed idle indifference. My harsh voice was gradually turning soft. I asked,

"What class have you read?"

"Eighth standard."

"Really? Wow! And you are doing this after reading so much."

She was without words. Amidst the loneliness of the valley, if I were the first man in her life she was pleading and expressing her desire, it would have been different, I thought. It would have mattered to me little whether Sunti was a *malua* girl or a *paana* Christian, whether she was scared of me or not. But I understood that it was different. She had lured many other travellers like me. She was a conqueror. As Napoleon won several kingdoms, she had conquered many hearts one after another.

I asked, "How many baboos you have rested with?"

With bare ridicule on her lips and vanity of victory in her eyes, she said,

"Oh! Many baboos."

"Really?"

"Do you think I am lying? Saltu baboo, Rabini baboo, Mesrot and many more."

There was ego of a victor in her voice. I went on staring at the Napoleon of this silent valley in surprise. Perhaps she was not lying. I wondered, if this nameless *malua* woman had given her strong beautiful body to those men for money only? Did she sell her attractive figure only for a blouse, a good saree or a bottle of scented oil?

I perceived soon that she was a threat to my manliness. Perhaps she had not yet experienced the pleasing pain in spite of her union with many men. Possibly those men were flitting memory just like stones in the path of her life. Her eyes acquired them, but mind didn't retain. ... I chided, "See Sunti! I will tell everything to the *Padri* Sahib."

With lips twisting, she said, "Go baboo. I have seen many *Padris*." After such retort, silence subjugated me. Before riding my bicycle to leave the place, suddenly I opened my purse. Sunti responded with a coquettish smile: "Do you want to give me money?"

"Don't you need?"

"I didn't call you to get money from you. Don't show me money. Go, baboo, go. You are a newcomer. That's why you are still afraid."

With my hurt manliness, I rode my bicycle. I could hear a woman's laughter from behind – a laughter as spontaneous as a mountain spring. The desolate valley resounded with the laughter. I thought that I should go back and slap her. If she were a girl from an aristocratic or educated family, I would have definitely done that.

Two days after the incident, while getting into my office chamber my doctor friend burst out, "Oh Jeevan baboo! What did I hear about you?" I assumed that he was joking. But he narrated his story and I was shocked. I said, "Me with Sunti?" I tried laughing loud. But it turned into a feeble laughter. I learnt that Sunti had spread a false story about me. I narrated the whole incident to my friend and I thought he believed in me. But I was not content. My character, honesty and reputation were at stake. In spite of my innocence, I felt ashamed. I supposed that all are watching me with scorn and hatred.

Afterwards, I crossed path with Sunti several times while visiting the market. But I didn't dare to look at her, though I wanted to. Whenever I caught her eyes, my eyes lowered against her straight forwardness.

Subsequently, I got my transfer order. I had developed

a bitterness for this place called Mala. My former infatuation with mountain forest and the earnest interest to know *kondh* tribe had vanished. I was glad to receive the transfer order. The day before I left, I was leisurely sitting outside my quarters on my armchair after lunch and recounting my days at Mala with a subtle sense of pain. To my utter surprise, Sunti was standing in front of me.

"Sunti."

That day her eyes were humble. There was no trace of impertinence in that countenance. I felt that she was a different Sunti. I sensed that a swift flowing mountain river had been suddenly tamed and turned immovable.

"You."

Sunti kept looking at me. In a trembling voice she said, "Baboo! Are you leaving the place tomorrow?"

"Yes. Why are you asking this?"

Sunti remained silent with a lowered head. I said, "I am leaving your Mala, Sunti. I will remember you a lot."

She looked at me with questioning eyes.

I answered, "Don't you believe?"

"How can I, baboo? Who am I to you?"

I turned away my face from her. Unexpectedly, I could feel someone's touch on my feet. I saw Sunti's head on my feet.

"Oh! Get up, get up; if somebody will see then…"

Irritated, I released my feet. I said, "I know everything. Leave. I am not angry with you." Sunti stood up. I firmly added, "Don't tell such lies to your baboos. Do you understand?"

Sunti nodded. Suddenly I remembered that she was literate. She had mocked at me, when I was giving her money. I enquired, "Sunti, don't you take money from baboos who visit you?"

"I take."

"Then why didn't you take money from me that day?"

Sunti stared at my face. I felt that she was pained by this question. I asked, "If you didn't want money, then why did you...?"

I was eager to know her mind. Somehow I convinced her to confess. From Sunti's disclosure I understood that she knew the mind of these so called gentlemen-baboos. She desired to marry an educated gentleman. Everybody was attracted towards her, but nobody accepted her as a wife. Frustrated, she had not stopped attracting them. Their aristocracy was not offended while enjoying her youth and beauty. She was surprised to find that their self-respect was not insulted by this act of enjoyment and this had increased her interest. She said, "How strange are the ways of these gentlemen? They will not accept me into their society, but how eager they are to embrace my attractive body in secret. What pleading in their eyes!" Sunti had felt a devilish happiness to watch this. When they approached her, she observed the twist of their muscles, the wildness of their eyes, yet they were terribly weak, helpless. Sunti enjoyed slaying their aristocracy.

Sunti remained silent for a while. I continued looking at her till I could believe it. I heard, "I thought you are also like them, baboo." I smiled a faint smile.

After standing there for some time, in an aching voice Sunti said, "I am going baboo; don't forget me. Do remember me."

I looked at her face in disbelief. What's this? Streams of tears were flowing from her eyes to wet her cheek – a symbol of her hurt womanliness. "Strange are the ways of women," I mused.

Sunti slowly walked away. She didn't look back. She crossed the gate. After she left, I asked myself: "Who is the vanquished? Sunti or I?"

❏

Two Friends

Pranabandhu Kar

Between the two *kondh* young women – Basali and Mudani – there was a deep friendship. Whether it is collection of *mahula* (butternut) or mango, reaping of crop or cutting of it – in all works one would find them together. It is a friendship since childhood. Both of them stepped into youth during the same season and even the same month. They often talked about their initiation into youth and its elation during leisure hour. The anxiety woven excitement of youth surfaced in their every work and talk. Their shy eyelids lowered when arrested the attention of young men.

Their village is a mile away from Udayagiri adjacent to the mountains. The two friends responded to the call of youth. They fell in love. One day Mudani got her man in the market. Mudani marked that a young man – unknown and unidentified – is following her and constantly looking at her. In the beginning Mudani felt discomfort and could not look at the man straight into the eyes. Gradually she mustered courage; her eyes met his eyes. The man smiled; Mudani smiled back at him. Basali chided, "Shall I call?" Mudani did not reply and continued standing there shyly. Basali called, "Hello, brother!" When the man came near,

Basali took a flower from Mudani's ear and put it on the man's ear and said, "Buy a *paan* (betel leaf) for my friend. What is your name brother?" The man replied, "Ratan" and stared at Mudani being captivated. Mudani happily roamed around the market with the friend of her youth. Basali sweetened the acquaintance of new lovers with her open laughter.

    Basali got the man of her heart when she was working as a labour for constructing the road. Many *kondh* young men and women were working on the site. They were carrying clay/soil to build the road. Many young men were digging the soil. The young men were carrying the soil and throwing it on the road. Ranjiga was digging soil. When he raised the shovel to dig, his muscles agitated. When Basali came to take the clay, she looked at him admiringly. Ranjiga filled clay in her pot and put it on her head. When Basali adjusted her saree, Ranjiga smiled at her. Shyly Basali leaves the place. Every time she went to pick the clay, the same sweet drama continued. Mudani marked it from a distance and joked with Basali, "So many people are digging the soil. Why do you bring it from Ranjiga only?" Basali smiled and said, "The mason has told me to bring clay from there. I will take his orders, not yours." Mudani smiled back. When they were taking rest under the tree, Basali told her mind to Mudani and both stared at the strong muscular body of Ranjiga. Ranjiga was digging in the hot sun, when all others were taking rest. Sweat flowed from his body. The two friends watched with silent amazement. Basali felt intoxicated. Mudani became her messenger.

    Ranjiga did not answer to Mudani and slightly smiled. The road work went on for days. Love cropped between Basali and Ranjiga. Ranjiga worked for Basali and Basali toiled for Ranjiga. When Basali did not go to work, Ranjiga felt weak. He got tired after a little labour. When Ranjiga did not come, Basali had the same feeling. The weight of soil broke her neck. She earned less that day.

The dream lives of two young women flew with immense love and happiness. They cherished and stored the moments of happiness and moved forward impatiently in hope of building their nest.

***

While collecting *mahula*, Basali said, "Friend! We will have our engagement on the same day."

"Engagement? Did not you hear that my man is going to work in the factory?" Mudani said.

Basali was agitated, "Will Ratan go to factory? Why did you agree to leave him?"

Mudani sighed, "Will he listen to me? What can we do? Men do whatever they want."

Basali said, "I will not let my man go."

Mudani retorted, "What do you mean by 'not let him go'? Ratan told me that Ranjiga has decided to go."

Basali stood shocked.

They had no wish to collect *mahula* that day. Both suffered the same heartache, same fear. *Mahula* dropped and covered their bodies, but they went on thinking about their imminent departure from their men.

This abrupt change in their situation within a short span moved their inexperienced soft heart. Evening approached. They could not sense it. Both Ranjiga and Ratan came to meet Mudani and Basali for the last time before going to Lahore. Both the friends had decided that they would neither talk nor dance with them. When Ranjiga and Ratan pleaded, they did not melt and said, "You did not keep our request. Why should we obey you?"

Ratan hugged Mudani and Ranjiga held Basali. Ratan

said, "You women will not understand what will happen if we stay here? You will eat only boiled dal. Many young men have gone – *paanas*, Christians. See how they are sending 40 to 50 rupees every month. They are bringing so many things for their women – perfume, scented oil, jacket, bangles, etc. What are we giving you?"

Basali angrily said, "Don't give those things. We do not need those. How shall we live without you?" Ranjiga brushed his cheek against Basali's cheek and said, "Shall we not come? Are we going to stay there forever?"

The warm touch of their men had weakened the two friends. The two young men could pacify them in a short time. Moon rose after a couple of hours of darkness. When they saw Mudani and Basali slightly smiling, they stood up and started playing the musical instrument (*khanjari*). The small *kondh* village sparkled with the clinging sound. Two or three more young women came out. They kept Mudani and Basali in the center and took their position. The dance started – the sound of bracelet along with the clinging sound of the playing instrument induced dreams in the mind of the young men and women of the hilly country. They forgot the pain. The aroma of *mahula* flower was coming from far. Ranjiga started singing a *kui* song.

"My fair woman! I'm going to a distant foreign country. Why are you worried about me? There is no smile on your moon face. Your hair has grayed. I will suffer if I remember your faded face in distant land. So, you bid me goodbye while smiling. The smell of *mahula* flower does not bring excitement in life today. The moonlight is spreading the cry of suffering."

The instrument of Ratan released inharmonious sound. The tears of pain sprang from Ranjiga's song. His throat choked.

The tears on the cheek of Mudani and Basali sparkled in moonlight. The sounds of their bracelets could not match the tune of the song. Basali and behind her Mudani ran into the house to suppress their sobbing. The sound of the instrument stopped. The song ceased. Both the young men went after them. That night they slept in tight embrace forgetting the impending separation. Next morning the honeyed desire and touch had smeared dreams on their face amidst the fear of separation.

***

After two days Mail and Serif bus was waiting for the war going *kondh* and *paana* young men in Udayagiri bazaar chowk. Ratan was walking with Mudani hand in hand and Ranjiga was holding Basali's hand. A big procession followed them. Many young women like Mudani and Basali were walking with their young men. There was tear in everyone's eyes. The atmosphere resonated with the lament of loved ones as the hills and roads of Udayagiri trembled. Ranjiga and Ratan sat near each other in the bus. Mudani and Basali controlled their tears and continued to watch them. As the bus departed, disappearing from view, the two friends were left alone with their shared anguish. By the banks of the Salki river, they wept for hours before finally returning home, their spirits drained from the weight of their sorrow.

The moving flourishing youth in them stopped as if a flowing river has stopped its course suddenly due to obstacles on its way. The sound of their loud laughter piercing the hills and the jungles was no longer heard. In the meantime, some fairs were held in nearby villages. With money attached to their waist, cap on head, wearing necklace and red blue cotton cloth, many young women of Mala holding their men's hand passed on before their eyes to the fair in groups with loud laughter, but it could not move the two friends. The two love-lorn hearts came closer to each other and got solace in staring at each other for hours.

***

Both of them came to Udayagiri post office in hope of a letter. They waited in the veranda of the post office. At 5:00 in the evening the mail bus came from Berhampur. Their expectation rose at the sound of the bus. Excitedly, they waited for the mail bag to reach the post office. This moment felt like eternity. To hide their excitement some bizarre conversation escaped their dry throat. The bag came. The peon opened the seal with a knife, poured the letters on the floor from the bag. The letters were stamped and distributed. Both watched each of these acts eagerly. Their heart beat faster, but they did not get any letter. Two painful sighs melted in the evening air.

Still, they came on time every day without any repentance or hopelessness. Many people gathered at the veranda of the post office, when the mails arrived – clerks, teachers, constables, peons and many others. Some people looked at them from the corner of their eyes and smiled, but they did not stop coming. No language or sign can be detected in the eyes of the two friends. They did not feel the presence of people around.

One day the post peon read loudly from inside the post office, "Batu Kanhar. Kumhari Kumpa." Basali rushed like an arrow, "Yes, yes, that's my brother. Give the letter to me. From where has it come?" The post peon said, "From Lahore." Illiterate Basali asked, "Laure?" The post peon ridiculed, "Yes, yes, Laure. Why are you so excited? Has your man gone to the war?" Basali blushed and replied with a smile, "Give me the letter. Don't talk rubbish." After catching hold of the letter in hand, Basali and Mudani ran towards the village breathlessly. They went to Batu.

When Batu opened the letter, he found two pieces of papers inside. The letters were written in Odia. Batu read hesitantly. On one sheet of paper was written in big uneven letters "Mudani" and on the other piece "Basali." He handed over the letters to both of them with a curved little smile.

Basali said with feigned anger "Oh! Can we read Odia? You read it."

Batu said laughingly, "Why should I read the letters of your men?"

Mudani and Basali uttered together, "We do not mind. Read it."

To raise their anxiousness, Batu said, "Which one should I read first – your's or Mudani's?"

Mudani grew impatient, "Oh! Why are you playing with us? Read whichever you wish to read."

Batu read Mudani's letter first hesitantly. Excitement of Basali and Mudani knew no bound. Batu read, "We came to Lauri well. Lauri city is feeling good. There is no house like Udayagiri here. Only big buildings. Many buses, electric lights are on the roads in the evening. I am well. I remember you. When I go, I will take soap, scent, jacket for you. Do you remember me?

Your man,

Ratan Mallik." (*incorrect grammar in the original writing to show they were less educated*)

Tears of happiness rolled down Mudani's eyes. Unrestrained expectation was visible on Basali's face. Her man would have written all these to her. He would have promised to bring soap and scent for her. Then Batu read Basali's letter. It had the same content. Only to the end was added, "Don't love any other young man. Your man, Ranjiga Kanhar." Both the friends swam in the flow of untold happiness. They resumed their day-to-day mundane life. When they received letter from Lauri (Lahore), they roamed around happily, staying aloof from the daily work. They shared their feelings and memories. Every time they talked about those, they seemed fresh.

One day a letter came. Ranjiga and Ratan went to Kohima in Assam where intense war was going on. The sensation of fear shook their lovelorn soft heart.

Several months ago, on that evening, there was a fair in Gracingia. Towards the end of winter last year, when spring was painting colors in nature, these two young girls had met their companions-for-ever. It had turned one year. Spring had returned – that day marked the first day of the Spring fair in Gracingia. It spread everywhere, indulging everyone in the festival of Spring – the old, the young, the children. The juice of *mahula* intoxicated them. The light of the full moon, the wind of spring aroused bodily desires in young men and women. There was no hesitation, no restriction. Fathers, mothers, brothers – everyone moved around the fair. Still, the young men walked away holding their women, and the women walked tightly holding their men's waists, just like pairs of free birds in the sky.

The festival came to an end. The young men and women moved in small crowds on the road. The happy laughter of two young lovers pierced hearts, audible from behind the bushes. This call of the Spring had no impact on Mudani and Basali.

In the morning both the friends were sitting in front of Basali's hut. They were breaking the mango seeds and collecting the inside stuff.

Mudani inquired, "Will you go to the fair?"

Basali responded, "Who will go? Why? There is no pleasure in going. Will you go?"

Mudani said, "There is no pleasure for you. Is there any pleasure for me?"

Basali sighed, "The letters have stopped coming."

Mudani speculated, "They don't get time, it seems."

❑

The Daughter of Niyamagiri

Rajat Mohapatra

There was only one king for the nine thousand nine hundred ninety nine *kondhs* (a tribe). The oldest *dangaria* (a person living in hills) among the indigenous mountain people of the area was called Niyama King. Sitting in the trunk of a tree with termite roaming on his beard, he implemented *niyama*, the rules; so he was named the Niyama King. The foremost rules in his kingdom were that nobody would starve and nobody would remain naked. Also, no one could cut trees or kill animals. The forest had given them everything. Nobody was allowed to sell the land. They would refrain from being shrewd and adopting the urban ways. Nobody would be suspicious of the other or betray others. Betrayal – a layer of sweet falsehood over truth – was considered the first sign of urban civilisation. The king had also declared that nobody was permitted to be educated the way town people were educated. He believed that such education led to the destruction of rural societies. Take for instance, reading newspaper meant to cut trees and buying books implied disappearance of forest. Similarly, using shoes meant killing of cows and wearing fur denoted death of sheep. Everyone obeyed and respected the king's rules. The life of *dangaria kondh* (the kondh tribe living in the Niyamagiri hills in the state of Odisha) was tied to many such rules known and unknown to others.

The king heard a girl crying one day. He beckoned to her and asked, "Daughter, why are you crying?" Sobbingly, the girl replied, "Father is beating me after drinking *handia*, country liquor."

"Don't you have a mother?"

"No."

"Where did she go?"

"I don't know. She left the house because father beat her."

"Don't cry. Now you are my daughter. No one will beat you."

Wiping her tears, the girl returned home. After that day no body dared even telling her anything. Everybody knew that every nook and corner of Niyamagiri, the mountain region, was under the rule of Niyama King and in his regime there was equality for all.

Soon the girl grew into a young woman. Her name was Jhumki. Her body was as smooth as the high hills. Everything about her – her eyes, ears, body and heart – was beautiful like nature. It was difficult to take one's eyes away from her. Bideshi (the foreigner) was following her from a distance since some days. He was captivated by her beauty and had a strong desire to come near her. He was impatient to know how she spent her day and night.

Jhumki stood out among the other *dangaria* girls. She appeared to be an inherent aspect of nature itself – seamlessly connected to the forest and the mountains. Her ancestors had inhabited the foothills for millennia, fostering the forest while being sustained by it in return. The deep hues of the Kondh people and the lush, verdant mountain forest harmonized perfectly, living in symbiosis with one another. Jhumki's ripened body gave the impression of inscription on black stone. Her round face with smooth cheeks, her watery eyes marked with kajal (kohl), the nose ring on her flat nose, her hair tied in a round bun decorated with wild flowers and pins, the necklaces hanging from her shoulders, the brass and silver rings adorning her ears, attracted the onlookers. She had blue tattoos on her forehead consisting of geometrical shapes. She had also got her name with three stars inscribed on her hand. These tattoos were very dear to Jhumki. Her mother had wished the name inscription to ensure that if the child was lost, she could be brought back to the mother.

The foreigner secretly followed Jhumki. The foreigner clandestinely trailed Jhumki as she went about her morning routine. As the sun emerged from behind the mountains, Jhumki bathed in the river. Along the riverbank, beneath the shade of an ancient banyan tree, stood a stone adorned with vermilion. Each day, Jhumki offered flowers and vermilion to this deity, bowing in reverence and whispering incomprehensible words. Upon rising, a silver coin would mysteriously drop from a tree branch above. She would collect it, knotting it into her saree with care, then discreetly stow it away in an old earthen pot. This ritual occurred daily, known only to Jhumki and Sukru, a trusted friend who provided protection and help in times of need. But soon the mystery of the coin became known to the foreigner too.

When Sukru was not nearby, the foreigner approached Jhumki and said, "You have got what I am searching for. Will you give it to me? I will give you whatever you want in return. I want to take the coins you have collected in exchange of two thousand rupees. You keep this one thousand rupee note today. I will pay the rest of the amount after taking the coins tomorrow. I am sure you have not seen such notes earlier." He handed a one thousand rupee note to Jhumki and explained, "Do you know the value of this note. This is worth a thousand coins you get in one thousand days. You will get two such notes. You can fulfil all your wants. You can buy anything and spend it according to your wish." Jhumki could not believe her ears. Staring at the foreigner, she said, "I will tell you tomorrow." The foreigner said, "I will wait for you tomorrow morning at this place. Come with those coins."

Jhumki agreed and came back home with the one thousand rupee note. Sukru met her on the way and they crossed the dark road together. The foreigner monitored from a distance. On the way, Jhumki smelled the paper note. She liked the strange scent it produced. The money in the pot lacked that fragrance. She dreamt of a wonderful future.

Next day, she handed over the half-filled pot to the foreigner and got another thousand rupees note. She carefully tied it to her saree. Then she took her bath, prostrated before the deity and waited; but there was no coin this time. She looked at the grass, looked around everywhere, but there was no sign of the coin. She returned home with a heavy heart. She consoled herself by thinking that though she lost the pot of coins, she had got notes of two thousand. She could get anything in exchange of it. Jhumki felt rich. The next moment, she felt confused. She knew that Niyama King was angry with her. That's why she didn't get any coin that say. Jhumki wanted to cry, "Can these two paper notes take the place of that pot of coins? It's impossible, just impossible." She conveyed it all to Sukru. Sukru comforted her, "I know everything. Don't be sad. Now you have a lot of money. What do you want to do?"

"Let's go and buy something from the market."

Both of them went to the market, but could not buy anything because the shopkeepers had not the capacity to return rest of the amount. It was not possible to spend the money even in the weekly market. They planned to go to the nearby town to get in exchange small notes which could be spent.

Next Saturday, they went to the town and were cheated. The swindler took a thousand rupee note from them and gave them ten fake hundred rupees notes. On return journey, the bus conductor refused to accept the fake note and forced them to get down. Luckily, Jhumki's childhood friend Lata was in the bus and she agreed to pay the bus fare. While walking down the village street, Sukru thoughtfully said, "We are *adivasis*; it is good for us to stay away from town people. Otherwise we will be doomed."

"Yes Sukru. You are right. Our village, our forest, our mountain, our river – they are for our well-being."

She smelled a hundred rupees fake note and murmured, "*Adivasis* can easily be cheated. What can they do?" She angrily tore all the notes and threw the papers in the air. She felt light. She had no money. She was tired and could no longer walk. She felt thirsty. Resting under a tree, she asked for water.

Sukru said, "Don't worry. I will fetch water for you. If I don't find water, I will come back with *handia* (country liquor). You stay here." Sukru went to bring water. The spring was not far, but that day there was no sound of falling stream and no trace of clear water.

Jhumki slept while resting. She dreamt. She visualised the foreigner coming with a bottle of water. He sprinkled water on her face and insisted her to get up. With closed eyes, Jhumki could clearly hear, "Get up Jhumki; get up. I am here with you. You will not be in trouble. Take some water, biscuit and cashew. Come and get into my car. I will take you towards civilization." Jhumki was thirsty. She felt water on her tongue. She went into a deep sleep. She sensed a close relation of man and mountain; the next moment she perceived a remoteness. Man delights in climbing the mountains. The mountain too revels in taking man into her lap. Sometimes man desires to shatter the mountain. But, standing at its foothill who has not felt insignificant. Man compares the steep rising hill with the broad captivating chest of nature. Nature is the best friend of human – the source of his strength and confidence. Nature nourishes life with food and water. Plants, leaves, flowers, fruits, mountains, birds and animals – all are indispensable for existence. Jhumki had well understood from her childhood that nature was her parents. When she wept on the stone outside her house, she could feel somebody comforting her. She felt a pair of consoling hands wiping her tears. Now deep sleep descended on her.

Amidst the silent green mountains, Jhumki's dream seemed to stretch from one horizon to the other. The mountain was filled with healthy green field puffing its chest and the spread of golden mustard flowers shining in fuzzy dreams. From the dense branches of the mango groves came the tweeting of the wood pecker. In another direction the fisherman could be seen in deep meditation. All these wove together a beautiful dream which nature only could create. Could fear exist in such a world? Behind the closed eyelids of Jhumki hid the rainbow world of dream. Leaning against the Siali creeper, she could feel the warmth of a mother's lap. She could envision dreams flying amidst floating clouds to the tune of celestial music.

Ah! She wished this beautiful reverie to continue. She yearned to see it with open eyes. She rose to sit. The receding glow of the sun from the west turned her face into a golden fairy. On her radiant body the tattoo created the illusion of filigree work. She discarded all she was wearing. She cast off her bangles, necklaces, ear rings, anklet and toe rings. Stark naked, she entered the stream to feel its depth. Her eyes gestured the foreigner to swim with her.

But the foreigner was engrossed in shooting the video of her crazy mermaid-like swim. He discerned that the young woman, ecstatic with happiness before a few moments, was being drowned, lost and hidden. The darkness of the western sky engulfed the water. His camera could no longer capture that deep darkness. He threw the camera into the water. He started walking like a man who had lost all sense of direction. He could experience the horror of darkness. A fear inducing voice intervened that darkness at intervals. He remembered Jhumki's face and marched forward.

❏

The Flying Fringe

Bhubaneswar Behera

Stirring the dense darkness of the night, the cock crowed, emitting a strange sound. The beginning of its call was long and melodious, but the ending was disappointing, reminiscent of much ado about nothing. It seemed as if, after uttering "cock-re-cock", the cock realized its mistake and hesitated to continue. However, the next moment, it appeared conscious of "what will people say" and completed the call anyhow, and seemingly felt relieved.

But that call was enough to awaken Bhainri; she suddenly woke up and, as she pushed Tulu, she said, "Wake up. It's already morning. The bus will arrive soon."

Tulu was sleeping on a miserable looking cot with a towel spread on it. While turning side, he opened her eyes to the darkness around and said, "Are you mad? It's still midnight. Why are you worried by a sleepy cock's untimely call? It must be the one-eyed cock of Govinda. The cock of Govinda is just like him. It's not morning yet. Go and sleep."

Bhainri was a little irritated, but gathering her bedclothes, she whispered, "Keep sleeping. If you miss the bus, you'll have to walk to Bhawanipatna. Whose legs will ache? The bus reaches Ratanguda by 7:00 am. Time won't wait for you. And Ratanguda is not a nearby place. You're still lazing around like a log; that's why nobody hires you."

Bhainri took palmful of water from the bottom of the earthen pot, sprinkled it on her eyes, and wiped her face. She then mixed some water with cow dung in another pot with a broader surface and sprinkled it in the courtyard. Perhaps wearing a new saree was not in her fate. Like a receding lotus, the new saree eluded her grasp as she attempted to catch it. But there was no use in blaming Tulu; she was also responsible. It would have been wiser to purchase the saree that Hari Bhulia (the weaver) had brought that day. The saree appeared sturdy and possibly durable. She could have used it for two years. It measured eight hands in length, sufficient to cover the chest and tie around the waist, with a width extending beyond the knee. It featured a beautiful fringe, one hand's width, with yellow embroidery across the body. Tulu dismissed it solely because it was a black saree with red fringe. He suggested that a red saree with a black border would look better on her. He brought two hands of red ribbon from the market for her and said, "Smear oil and turmeric on your body, wear this saree, adorn your hair with this ribbon, a silver comb, and two bunches of *kurei* flowers. When you walk, swaying your hips, all the young men in this area will swoon at the sight. I can guarantee it; Otherwise, I'll change my name from Tulu Shabar; I swear to God." A smile unknowingly spread across Bhainri's face. Despite his laziness, he loved her dearly. Hari Bhulia had set the price of the saree too high, she thought. She had remarked, "Eighteen rupees is too much for the black saree. Reba had got exactly the same saree from Habaspur market in fourteen rupees." Hari had sarcastically replied, "Fourteen rupees for such sarees.

One may give you looking at your beautiful face. Touch this saree – see the texture and the stitches. It'll become smoother and thicker with each wash. This isn't just any ordinary saree; it's a Bhulia (weaver) saree." He added, "You try this; it'll simply slip off your chest." "Shameless," she retorted, "Give it for fifteen rupees." He insisted, "Not a penny less than seventeen rupees." Tulu was angry. He declared, "Take your saree back; there are plenty like it in Habaspur market. I'll get her a red saree for fifteen rupees; and if you want, I can get one for you too."

Within seven days Hari Bhulia hiked the price of the black saree to twenty-one rupees in Habaspur market. Someone else had brought a red saree for twenty-three rupees. Tulu came back empty handed from the market as the price was lower in the village. However, yesterday, Hari Bhulia again came to the village and raised the price of the black saree to twenty-three rupees.

"Twenty and three! Have you dipped your hands in butter?" Tulu muttered, "He thinks that we have neither seen the world nor do we know about it. Go to Nabarangpur; nobody will pay attention to your saree. In Bhawanipatna, even the red saree will cost less than twenty rupees, at best one rupee less than twenty. The bus fare will cost two rupees to go and two rupees to come back. How much in all? One less than twenty, twenty, twenty and one, twenty and two." He started counting with his fingers: "One rupee I can spend on buying cream and face powder for Bhainri. Why should I give twenty-three rupees to this Bhulia?" Tulu decided that he would set for Bhawanipatna the next dawn. He would enjoy the bus ride, see the town, and roam around the market.

Bhainri remembered that she had to arrange rice for Tulu – he had to cook and eat on the way two times a day for two days. But Tulu insisted that he could not cook on the way; he would eat at a hotel. Somebody said that one could have a plate full of rice along with the dal (lentil), and curry in just half one and a half rupees. They also offered a second helping of rice for free. One could go on eating till the stomach was full, only in one and a half rupees.

"But only one meal costs one and a half rupees. He had to eat four times," thought Bhainri, "the last meal he can have at home; he should not take money for it." She could not calculate how much everything would cost. If they did not have sufficient money in the box, then… Bhainri went into the house in a hurry. She lit the oil lamp using the flicker of a straw. She brought down the earthen pot from the rope hanger and took out a bamboo box. She kept the box near the oil lamp and started straightening the notes to count. She counted with her fingers – four, two more, one, five…twenty and five. All the coins put together made two rupees more. That much in all. She divided the money – twenty-one for the saree, two and two for bus fare to and fro, and hotel… She would give him a sear of rice, four onions, some salt, and two green chilies. She would put everything in a brass pot along with the money and she would tie it tightly with a towel so that there would be no fear of losing it.

Did she do the right thing by buying this silver pot? Tulu kept insisting not to buy such things as he considered these a waste of money. He wanted to collect money to repay the loan of the money lender which he had taken during his marriage. But not buying the silver pot would not have solved the problem; only the interest amounted to forty-six – two twenties and six. They could have repaid the amount if they had stayed in Nabarangpur. But that sardar (head man) with the moustache... Bhainri trembled in fear, whenever she remembered that sardar.

The villagers were heading to work to dig a pond. Bhainri insisted that they would also go. Tulu's father did not agree. He said it was a distant land, and she was a newly married bride. It would be risky for her to go. In the village, everybody knew her. There was no fear. But it was different in a distant place. Nobody would be there to support in times of danger or need. But Bhainri was adamant. She said, "Your son cannot work as a laborer. Whatever ancestral land we got is not adequate to sustain both of us. There is an additional burden of a loan from the *mahajan*, and the festivals like Rathayatra and Nuakhai. We have to buy clothes to cover our bodies also. If I were not working as a laborer, your son would have died of hunger. And now you're telling me that I am a newly married bride."

The old man was angry at the retort. His second wife rushed to beat her. But Bhainri was not to be tamed. She said, "Do you want to beat me? Just try and see. Don't you know that I am the daughter of this village?" Knowingly she talked to herself aloud, "She has come from somewhere and forcibly acquired everything. She has broken the hearts of both the father and the son. Now she's trying to beat me. Don't I have strength in my hands?" Tulu's stepmother was tamed that day.

They walked to Nabarangpur as there was no money to pay the bus fare. They enjoyed the whole journey. After reaching their destination, they could get rice and wheat along with three rupees per person per day. It was not even a month when the gaze of the moustachioed Sardar fell on her. He constantly followed her. One day, he said, "If you work for one or two hours in the house of the contractor in the evening, then...You go to the contractor to work for one or two hours in the evening with your daughter." Her mind revolted.

The next day, Hadua's mother tried to persuade her: "It is a matter of 1-2 hours only, why don't you go? The contractor is a good man. But he is furious when he gets angry. When that girl from Sundergarh said no to him, nobody could find her husband." She added, "They are big people. They will gift sarees and ornaments, if they are satisfied." She wanted to tell Tulu to attack the old man with the axe. But she belonged to her own village. Tulu was saying that he would see the sardar. But that day before the evening, Bhainri forced Tulu to come back in fear that they might kill him. She said, "I know about your strength and intelligence. But I will not send you to the demon." Shortly after, they found a bus to return to their village.

Again, a cock cried, "Cock-re-cock." A response echoed from another end of the village. People began to stir, and various noises filled the air, bringing the village to life. Tulu could no longer sleep. He emerged from his dwelling, greeted by the sight of the morning sky with the bright morning star descending on the horizon, accompanied by the murmur of human voices in the village. The rumble of the village cart rolling along the road signaled that the day had already commenced.

***

Before morning Tulu had reached near the tea stall of Ratanguda bus stand and kept his belongings on a bench. Despite the temptation to indulge in a hot cup of tea and sip it on a plate until he sweated, he remembered the caution of Bhainri. He simply greeted the owner of the tea stall, "*Juhar* uncle," without placing an order. The uncle also noticed the limited availability of milk in the shop compared to the increasing number of customers expected upon the arrival of the bus. He refrained from asking anything specific and casually inquired about whether the village experienced rain the previous night. While engaging in conversation with the villagers about the potential impact of weather on the crops, Tulu could hear the sound of horns from a distance and positioned himself near the road, shouldering his belongings in preparation to board the bus.

As the travelers disembarked from the bus to have tea, he carefully boarded. The conductor informed that the bus fare to Bhawanipatna would be 2 rupees 30 paise. Tulu requested to take one and a half rupees and then offered an additional 25 paise as fare, but the conductor explained that bargaining was not allowed in government buses. Tulu argued that the forest guards, the police constables, the village *patwaris,* and even the panchayat secretaries allowed bargaining for their dues, so why not the bus conductor? However, the conductor simply glanced at Tulu and turned away. As the driver announced the departure of the bus, Tulu stepped down and began walking towards Junagarh. He still held out hope that the conductor would demand an additional 25 paisa and allow him to board, but the bus departed, leaving behind a trail of dust as it gradually vanished from sight.

Junagadh was only 10 miles away. He found company on the way. It wasn't tiring for him, as another attraction awaited in Junagadh – a meal at the hotel. He was not disheartened to learn that the rate had increased from one rupee fifty paise to two rupees due to the rising price of rice. He ordered two plates of rice with a little lentil soup (dal) and curry, and still asked for a third plate for free. The hotel owner became insecure of his business.

The bus fare from Junagadh to Bhawanipatna cost one rupee fifty paise. Due to overeating, he was without power to move. Without any objection, he paid the bus fare, occupied a comfortable seat, and soon started sleeping. At Bhawanipatna, he found the home of a distant aunt to stay. Tulu was happy to get free accommodation and dinner. The aunt was also glad as she found someone to narrate the incidents of the village, to cut the log and get containers filled with water from the roadside tap.

The next day was Tuesday market. Tulu ate some fermented watered rice served by the aunt and went out to buy a saree. When he was crossing Gandhi Chowk, someone was shouting, "Pay one rupee and get two lakh rupees. Who knows what fortune has stored for you? Buy lottery ticket for one rupee only. What is the value of one rupee in today's world? You cannot even buy a packet of cigarettes with it. But if fortune favours you, you can get two lakhs with one rupee. A beggar may become a millionaire."

Tulu was drawn to the fortune seller. He asked him, "How could one get two lakhs by paying one rupee? The fortune selling man examined Tulu and said, "Buy a ticket for one rupee. Do you see those tall buildings? When you win two lakhs, you will live in such a house." He wanted to buy a ticket, but he remembered Bhainri's advice. Before he started from home, she had said, "Look, don't waste money."

After he crossed the statue of Budharaja, he found the big market where all the things of the world had assembled. The sellers sat in rows with their spread to sell. There were heaps of rice, various dals, potatoes, onions, piles of okra, and brinjal being sold. Dried fish was also being sold – just roast in fire one piece of it and you can eat a bowl of watered rice with it. He had heard someone saying that one could buy everything except parents in town. He was actually right. One required money only.

Suddenly he started walking fast behind someone: "Hey...oh! Saree seller... stop, stop. Show me that saree. It is exactly like the saree of Hari Bhulia. What is the price?"

The saree seller smiled and asked, "Tell me about the length, the width and the design of the saree you need, then only I can tell the price."

Tulu selected a red saree and checked its border and its length by holding it from his waist and enquired, "How much will it cost?"

The saree seller answered, "Twenty-seven – twenty and seven."

"What do you say? It costs only seventeen rupees in our Habaspur market."

The saree seller laughed. He showed a short five hands black-colored saree and said, "It must be like this."

Tulu argued that it was not like that; rather, it was like the saree he had chosen. The saree seller extended his hand to collect the saree from him and moved forward without giving any reply.

There were hoards of sarees in the market. Tulu went from seller to seller and at last selected an eight handed red saree with black border and yellow embroidery work. The seller started from 23 and came down to 20 and said, "Pay now. I am selling you at a cheaper price." Tulu thought that the price might be two rupees less than 20 and he was being cheated. He made his excuses by saying, "I will just come back from my friend," and he went toward the goat, cow and bullock market.

He thought that he would come back after some time and bargain the saree for seventeen rupees. The big and small, fat and thin goats were tired to the rope and bleating, "Baa, baa." He asked the price of one of them. The seller said, "Seven twenties and ten." Tulu lifted the goat with both of his hands and murmured, "It cannot be more than 15 to 16 kg… Seven twenties and ten? Is it a goat or a bullock?"

A little further, bullocks in pairs were standing. He asked the price of a bullock. While looking at another person, the seller answered, "Eight-twenty." "Not bad," thought Tulu. He put his hand on the bullock's back and it looked back in anger. His hand had barely touched the bullock's tail and it kicked him. "Old bullock," remarked Tulu. The seller ridiculed, "Old bullock? What are you saying? It has not worked even for two years. It has walked a long distance. So, it looks tired. It can work for at least six years more."

Tulu nodded his head as if he knew everything. "Still," Tulu asked, "Will you sell in six twenties?" He was thinking of disposing his old bullock and buying a new one like this. It was better to know the price.

The seller looked with open eyes and asked, "Are you talking of six twenties or six hundred?" Tulu was confused. He could not determine what to say and made his way out of the bullock market. It was getting late. He should purchase the saree now. The weavers would be tired by now by roaming in the market and would sell at a cheaper price. When he came back to the saree market, he did not find any saree seller. Where did they go? He saw an auto-rickshaw at a distance and a heap of sarees near it. Tulu hurried to the place and when enquired, he discovered that those belonged to Ramahari Seth. Tulu was about to put his hand on one. Someone shouted, "Will you steal it?" Tulu clarified that he would buy a saree and he has selected one. The man replied, "Then go to the shop of Ramahari Seth after one hour."

***

The man sitting on the mattress with a big belly must be Ramahari Seth, Tulu thought. Tulu described, "Yellow embroidery in red saree, black border, *bhulia* saree, eight handed with black and yellow fringe."

Sethji ordered, "Ram Bilas! show him the saree." He was shown four sarees of different colors. Tulu touched the red one, and confirmed, "I will take this saree." Sethji announced the price, "Twenty-seven."

Tulu said that he had bargained the same saree for one rupee less than twenty. The seller declared that bargaining is not allowed in his shop; things have fixed prices. But he called, "Ram Bilas! Bring that red shining saree of Biswa Rupak Mills – seven hands."

Ram Bilas threw 4-5 pieces of saree in front of Tulu. Sethji said, "This saree is beautiful. It will look good on your girl… What is the complexion of the girl?... Yes, it will look good… where is your house? Oh! Sunadungri? What is your caste? … Shabar…Why didn't you tell that? I know everyone? Jara Shabar, Angad Shabar, Bali, Sugri...."

Tulu said, "Sir, the name of my grandfather is Angad."

"Yes, I know. He has bought sarees from my shop so many times. Take this red saree."

"Sir, the color of the saree is beautiful, but it is too thin." He measured the length and said, "Six hand long. The fringe cannot be tied to the waist. The width also is only knee length."

Sethji smiled and said, "Oh, ignorant Tulu. Is your bride fat?"

Tulu replied in an irritated tone, "Why should she be fat?"

"Then," Sethji continued, "What would you do with seven or eight hand long saree? Have you watched a film? Don't you see how the modern girls wear saree? Knee length. It looks good if the calf is visible. No one ties the fringe to the waist. Thin red saree on the waist...A hand long fringe on yellow blouse... The fringe will fly with the wind. She will walk shaking her waist. Have you listened to the song? The fringe is flying in the wind...See how she walks, the lady... Take this... Obey my words... Ram Bilas, bring that yellow blouse. Show him the box of powder, the small soap, and the plastic comb and golden hair clips... See Tulu, I am giving you ribbon, comb, and clips for free. Take all these, you are our old and known customer."

Tulu asked with a smiling face, "Sir, how long will this saree last? Will it last till a year?"

"One year? It will last for two years if properly used. It should not get damaged by any bamboo or branch. Tell your girl to sit carefully."

"What is the price?"

"Price? It will be one rupee less than twenty, but you can give two rupees less than twenty, as you are known to me."

Tulu is watching like a snake snatched off its teeth, looking at the flute of snake charmer from a box. It was not distinct whether it was a glance of happiness, wonder, fear, anger, or enchantment. Slowly, he kept the saree, blouse, powder, soap, ribbon, comb, and clips in his towel and put a tight knot. He counted all the notes he had and handed them over to Sethji. He had only five rupees and fifty paisa in his hands now.

***

The man was shouting, "If it is in your fate, you can get two lakhs with only one rupee." Tulu went there. Two persons were talking: "How a person from Balangir..." Tulu handed over one rupee and said, "Give me a ticket." The ticket man asked, "One or two? If your wife's fortune is better than you..." Tulu handed over another rupee, took two tickets and carefully tied it in his towel.

He ate at a hotel in Junagadh to his heart's content, boarded the bus, and reached Junagadh. The sun had already set down the horizon by the time. He did not have a single paisa. He had to walk to his village. If he had only twenty-five paisa, he could have reached soon and shown Bhainri her the saree, blouse, soap and powder in the evening. But he had no money left. Without delay, he started towards his village with big steps.

Two persons came out swinging out of the cottage near the canal close to Ratanguda. Tulu remembered that he had not used the rice he carried. He could get a bottle or a half bottle of .... He directed his steps towards the cottage.

When he reached Ratanguda, the evening bus had started for Junagadh. With his body full of dirt, swelling face, foam from his mouth, moving from one side of the road to the other side, Tulu reached the bus. He showed the two tickets and shouted, "Oh government! How much does this bus cost?"

The bus driver smiled at Tulu: "This bus costs one lakh rupees. Will you buy it?"

Tulu hiccupped, "One lakh? Take five less than one lakh."

There was a man who seemed to know Tulu; he was trying to hold his hands, perhaps, to lead him to his home. Tulu pushed his hand away and told the driver, "Oh government, will you sell for five rupees less than a lakh? See here, two lakhs... take this... return the rest of the money."

When the bus left, Ghenu of Sunadungri pulled Tulu's hand to make him cross the village road. Perhaps, Bhainri had got the news. She rushed to the road. When Tulu saw

Bhainri, he tried to dance, showing her the two tickets, but fell on the ground. Before he was conscious, he said, "Oh girl! see, two lakh rupees. Take it. Building... bus... red sarees...hick... the fringe flies in the wind... hick."

❏

The Burning Mountain

Gayatri Saraf

That night also Sarojini was writing a story for long hours. She was ruminating on the climax of the story. She was scribbling something, then scratching it. Suddenly she felt someone entered into her room like wind. She was taken aback. She instantly withdrew from the world of stories and looked around the room. She could see the shadow of a woman. The woman stood beside her in the darkness and sharply asked, "You write stories, right? But what do you write? About whom do you write? Have you ever written about a woman like me? Does woman mean someone like you – an urban educated woman? People like us who live in broken cottage, insufficiently clad in a torn saree, dying every minute, then surviving any how – are we women? For us it is a costly world. I told it to make you understand. Have you ever seen people like us? Have you ever been to a village to feel our poverty, our suffering? Have you ever told the story of our starvation?"

That sharp voice wet with sorrow and the arrows of words pierced Sarojini's heart. She was injured. She could not look straight at the direction. Looking at the writing paper, she closed the pen with the cap and asked, "Who are you? What do you want to say?"

A warm voice uttered, "My story. I want to tell you, my story. I know you will not ignore me. You will listen to me and tell it to others. You read my life and write your story. I will tell you the suffering of my body in my language. You tell it in the language which can be understood by people of your society – those who have abundance of food, water, light and many more things."

Sarojini listened to the voice of the shadow drenched in emotions. It continued the story:

"What is there to talk about my identity? Is there an identity for us? Yes, I have a name. My name is Ukia Burme. Ukia means light, but there is no ray of light in my life. It begins in the darkness and ends with it. I was silent with my suffering. Before whom would I make my claims, complaints? Who will understand my plight? It melts with the dust of our village street. But today I am burning with jealousy. I'm envious not of your fairy life. I am jealous of another woman like me. I am jealous of her name, her fate. She is Premasheela. She died of starvation. Death made her fortunate. A lot of hustle and bustle ensued her death. You all recognized her. You saw her photograph with her children. But do you know me? Have you come across me and my daughter in any newspaper? There was no camera, no newspaper, no reporter to listen to my story. So tell me, whether I should be jealous of Premsheela's fate or not? Premsheela belongs to our adjacent village. Village does not mean here the village you see in your primary school book. We do not have green forest, blue mountain or a flowing spring. Once upon a time there was a forest full of trees, flowers and fruits. It was a forest with fruits like *kendu, mahula, chara, kusuma*. Their sweet fragrance filled the forest. When we were hungry, we used to go to the forest and eat to our heart's content. We came back with bundle of wood on our heads. Forest was our mother. She had opened up her treasure to satisfy our hunger. It provided us shade. Its air wiped our sweat. It helped pouring rain on our field. But people cut the trees. It wounded our chest, stomach and backbone. We lost our mother. The aroma of forest plants and its products was lost from our village. After that rain was not visible in our sky. The earth dried. There was no crop. It made no difference to the rich. They borrowed from banks, dug wells and bought pumps. They survived. Their field had crops. We looked at the evasive sky, dry earth, and burning mountains. Land turned barren. Dust replaced the smiling crops. What would we do? What would we eat? How would we live?

My husband Samara became a servant in the house of a *sahukar*, the money lender. The *sahukar* made him work more and paid less. That money could not satisfy the hunger of our family – we two and our daughter. We were half fed. There was no other work available in the village. There was no scope to opt for another job to get more money and a full meal every day. This flight was not ours only. This was the sorrow of many Ukias and Samaras. One day the *sahukar* announced, "Samara! I no longer need a servant." Samara came and stood helpless in front of me. I consoled him. He asked for water. I said that there was no water in the tube well. Water poured from my eyes. He cursed the earth, the sky, the hunger, the thirst, and his fate. A handful of rice and a pot of water became a dream for us.

We, the starving dreamers, went to the headman's building. The building smelt of something. Someone said, it is the smell of rice. Another said, it is the smell of money. Someone else uttered, it is the smell from the body of the head man. We pleaded, "Give us work, give us food." The headman was irritated. He shouted, "Leave, leave my place. The hungry lots – always begging…" Someone said, "To whom shall we tell, if not to you. You know and see the government. You tell them our story."

"Yes, yes. I will tell… you go now."

We came back. We did not know whether he conveyed our suffering to the government or not. We did not know where did the government stay, how much hunger qualified for rationed rice from the government, how many dried ponds led to the digging of tube wells. Several questions crossed my mind. Why did nobody care for us? What were we asking for? Sugar, molasses, dal, vegetable, wheat flour or oil for hair, a meal a day and water to wet the throat. We were not asking this for free. We wanted work. We would work and earn to eat. I heard that last year there was a flood somewhere. It destroyed houses. People starved homeless. Every heart cried for them. Aeroplanes came to drop food parcels. We were also suffering from drought, from hunger. We were not asking for clothes; even food would be sufficient for us. But nobody felt for us. No aeroplane flied. Why did nobody listen to us?

One person had listened to us. One day he came with a bundle of notes. We had not seen so many notes together earlier. How could one get so much of money. To watch that bundle of notes was a rare and amazing thing for us. He said, "if you want, you can also have this."

Someone asked, "There can be no connection between us and the bundle of notes. Did the government send you for us?"

"Silent! Don't talk about the government. My master has sent me. He heard about your hunger. He has been kind to you. If you are willing, then come with me. I will take you to Andhra. You will make bricks and get money. Then you can buy rice and many more things. You can buy saree, blouse, and bangles. Come and register your name. Take money in advance."

After listening to him many felt rain on the dried earth of the village. Leaves appeared on the dying plants. My husband Samara looked at me. Taking my daughter in my arms, I said, "Andhra is a distant place. We will not go. You go to the town and work as a laborer or make brick. Come back in the evening."

In sad tone Samara said, "In town one does not make brick. One does not get work as a laborer every day. Now there is shortage of water in town as well. Anyhow we have to survive. We have to leave the village to survive. This village and this government have cheated us. How long can we stay in our land with empty stomach. One can count your bones. Our daughter is asking for rice. I am young, but there is no strength left in my body."

I looked at Samara, then shifted my glance at my daughter. I looked through the hunger in their stomach. How long can one survive without food? I looked at my torn cloth. One can go out with empty stomach, but not without cloth on the body. For cloth, for the stomach, we have to leave the village. Food and cloth come first. Then only one can think of the motherland. I said, "Go Samara. Register your name and my name too. Both of us will go. We will toil and survive. One who gives us food will be our savior. We will leave this place, this village." Our names were registered. That man gave us some money. It filled our palms. He said, "I will come after two days. Be ready with your things."

Life sprouted from every cottage. Smoke of the hearth was visible for those two days. Samara went to purchase a pot and a couple of pans from the nearby village. I dreamt of many things at the sight of those cooking pots.

Rice would boil in it. The smell of boiling rice would fill the house. I would serve rice in those two pans. Samara would eat, my daughter would eat too. She would laugh and play. But some disbelief lucked in my mind. Would such days really come in our life? We started our journey from Kantabanji after two days. My daughter cried with fear while getting into the train. My heart beat faster. The train took us through an unknown route. We left our village, land, field and pond behind. The contractor warned us, "Don't tell anybody where and why you are going. Did you understand? If someone asks, tell that you are going to visit relatives." Morning came after night. We reached our destination at lunch time. Many people like us alighted from a truck near the brick factory. The place was bigger than our village. Crowds of men and women were seen. There were rows of small cottages. The contractor counted us and handed over us to the master. We could not understand what they discussed. The contractor vanished after that. The master came to us and talked to us separately, "Go and build your house with the advanced money. You will be given work after three days. I want perfect work. If I am not satisfied with your work, I will drive you out." When we were thinking about how to build a cottage, a person came and asked us what type of house we wanted to make. He said, "Come to my shop. I will find bamboo jute bags, tall leaves, rope and everything you need. You can find rice and food also." We built a cottage with gunny sacks; tall leaves made the roof. That was our dream cottage, a cottage where goddess Lakshmi lived. Here we could find rice to eat every day. We got work after three days. First, we got a demand of one thousand bricks. I worked in mud. Samara made bricks. Our daughter was watching this sitting near me. She was playing with other children. I felt very tired in the beginning, then it became a habit. The master often came to supervise. One day he came near me and asked, "Are you new? Have you come from Kantabanji? Only you two have come or someone else is with you? What is the name of your husband? Is he making bricks?" My legs and body were shaking. While jumping on the mud, I answered all his questions. He said, "Good! Work hard." I worked hard always. When I returned home in the evening, I felt tired. I wanted to sleep, but when I saw the cooking pot and rice my strength returned. I cooked hot rice and served it to both of them. I also ate. I thought, "If we eat like this, we can live long." Tears of happiness flew from my eyes, while eating. I watered the rest of the rice to eat in the morning. We needed to eat to work the whole day. One day after dinner while wiping his hands in towel, Samara said, "The master is not happy with my work. He is saying that I cannot make good bricks and I am lazy. That day I heard that the master has a secret chamber. If somebody disobeys him or he is angry with somebody, he keeps him in chain in that secret chamber and beat." After my daughter slept at night, I came close to him and said, "You work well. If you are there, I have everything in life."

One day the master came to me and said, "It is the work of women to cook at his home and the one who cooks, gets food and saree. Today is your turn. So, you have a holiday today from this brick work." I thought of him as a God at that time. He understood the suffering of poor. He gave work, food and cloth. I washed my hands and went to his house with my daughter. He was such a big man. Would he really eat food cooked by me? Could I cook the items of food he ate? But it was his order. So, I had to cook. If I did not obey, he would keep me in chain in that secret chamber. What would be the condition of Samara and my daughter after that. I went to his house. I washed the utensil and started sweeping the floor. My daughter was sitting. The master came. He observed me from toe to tip, gazed at my chest and burst out, "God has rightly made you poor. Come to the kitchen. Do you know cooking." I was scared and said, "I know cooking rice and dal." "But we eat meat. Rice and Dal cannot satisfy our hunger," he said and then laughed loudly. He came closer and caught me. Touching my cheek, he said something which I could not comprehend, but I understood that he was not speaking of good things. He had not called me to cook. He had evil things in his mind. I used all my strength to release myself from him. Taking my daughter, I came back to Samara. Sadly, I said, "I thought of the master as God, but he is not a good man. Also, he called me to cook, but tried to violate my izzat (honor). Let's go from here. The master is hungrier than us." Samara's eyes burnt like fire. With muddy hands, he said, "You go home. I will go to the master's house." Watching his fiery eyes, I feared: "You do not go to him. Can we fight with him? We will go away silently at night." Samara did not listen to me. In burning anger, he went; but never returned. I waited. It was lunch time, but he did not come back. My heart beat faster as the master might have kept Samara in the secret chamber. He was the king of the area. His wish reigned. I was scared, but stepped out of the cottage with my daughter. I went to the master's house and summoning courage called aloud, "Samara, Samara." Reply came from the house, "Your Samara is a notorious man. How dared he throwing mud on my face? He slapped me with the hands to whom I have given work. I have chained him." I cried, "Please, release him, Baboo. We will go away."

"Okay! I will release him in the morning. You come inside and eat. Feed your daughter also. Sleep on the bed like a queen. Go with Samara in the morning. You will get saree and money also."

I turned back as if deaf, but two messengers from the God of death stopped me. One took my daughter from me forcibly and the other pushed me into the room and locked the door. I shrieked loud, but it disappeared in darkness. The knot of the saree loosened and the dropping coins clinged. The master did not make me queen on the bed, but made me a beggar. There was no rescue after that. After Yama, the two messengers of Yama came. I fainted. When I gained consciousness, I heard that Samara had escaped.

I felt that I would faint again. With much effort, I stood up. I wore my saree. My daughter was sleeping without caring for anything. How could that innocent soul sense what her mother had lost and what her father has lost. I saw that his men were busy searching for Samara. I was forgotten. I came out with my daughter. There was darkness all around. Where should I go? Should I go back to the cottage? Samara would not be in the cottage. So, what would I do here? Should I return to the village? But where was the way? Which train would take me to Samara, to my village? I started walking. I left the Lakshmi cottage along with the pots and the pans behind. I left the mirror which showed the face for the first time. An impulse impelled to go and collect that wealth, but I did not turn back. I lost my real wealth in this land. This land also took my Samara away from me. I was crying at heart. My eyes turned into stone. Then, I crossed the fire of many brick factories and many rivers of sorrows to reach Kantabanji. From there, I went to my village, my cottage. My stone eyes now overflowed with tear. What should I do now? What should I eat? How would I feed my daughter? Again, I came face-to-face with that hunger, that thirst. I had no strength left in me to fight. The villagers came to me and asked, "Where is Samara? Why did you come alone?"

With an unknown hope, I said, "He will come. He will come with money." But there was no hope, no light in my life. He did not come. My daughter did not stop crying. She continued to cry for rice. Love had withered within me, replaced by callousness. Frustration and anger welled up, and I lashed out at her, blaming her for my loss of dignity and my Samara. I stayed hungry. I bitterly cried, "You witch! You ate your father. Now eat your mother. Drink my blood. Eat my meat. Don't dream of rice. Don't even think of it. Why weren't you born in a rich house? You found my home only." Her helpless cry filled the air.

I burnt in rage. I took her to the zamindar's house. I told his wife, "Keep her and give me some money. I sell her to you. Shall I tolerate my hunger or her? Take her and save me." The wife of the landlord took my daughter and gave me twenty rupees. I cried a lot. My daughter ran to me, held me tightly and cried. The weight of her tears neither tear the sky nor the land, but it pierced my heart. The veins of my body tore to pieces. The landlady snatched my daughter's hand. Once upon a time, I used to sell fruits. That day, I sold my daughter, my blood. With that money, I went to the shop with unashamed feet.

I bought sweets and fried stuffs and came back to the cottage. I would eat everything. I would eat the leaves, the paper, the dust, the earth, the whole village, the entire district and the whole state, entire India even. The earth shook. The heaven whirled. I sat down. The fried snacks and the sweets shattered all around. Standing against the wall, I called out, "Daughter, daughter, come, come and eat snacks. Come and eat sweets… hope… dream."

But where was my daughter?

Where's her cry, her tears, her hunger, her calling me mother?

I could not listen to anything.

I could not see anything. Darkness. Only darkness prevailed.

The words were lost.

Language, emotion... everything was lost.

Sarojini was worried. Kindly, she said, "Ukia! Tell me, what happened after that."

But who? Where? When?

Sarojini was knocking on the wall. There was silence everywhere. Only the voice of night was heard. Where did Ukia go? She sought for her – inside the house and outside it, in the newspapers.

Where could she go?

She is here, she is there. She is a terrible truth – very far from us. She is in the chasm of barren land, on the chest of the burning mountain, in the cry of a starving stomach. But the eyes lack the courage of to see and acknowledge this. That is why it is declared that she does not exist.

❏

Rebati

Tarun Kanti Mishra

The long-distance passenger train was slithering into the platform like a starving snake. The evening star had started twinkling in the north east at the same time. Like the scattering birds from the branches of a burning forest, the passengers got down the coaches of the train. It was the last station. The train would not go further; still they worried to get out of the coaches.

A man came out of the crowd of a second-class coach and a girl of twelve or thirteen years was holding his hand. The girl had never travelled by a train before; she had never before seen the railway station of a big city; even the large crowd was unknown to her. The girl held the father's hand tightly and whispered, "Papa! I want to go to the toilet."

"Again. You had gone to the toilet only a moment before."

"I had gone, but it did not happen."

The man straightened the pleats of his dhoti, opened two buttons of his shirt and said, "Oh! It's too hot in Calcutta." It was less hot outside the station. The girl looked relaxed after passing the urine behind the old wood cabin. The girl asked, "Papa! Is there really a big zoo in Calcutta?"

"Yes, there is a zoo. There are many other things in Calcutta like Howrah bridge, airplane, tramcar, big buildings. And you will see everything."

"What is tram, Papa?"

There was no need to describe. In front of their eyes a tram passed with sound of horns towards Howrah bridge.

"Wow! I had not seen something like this earlier."

The man laughed loud in acknowledgement of the daughter's ignorance. Coming from Surangipadar village of Kalahandi district of Odisha the girl had not seen and known many things. The list of the unseen and unknown was too long just like the huge platform of Howrah station.

"Papa! I am hungry."

The girl looked at a breakfast stall greedily.

"Hungry? You just had half a rupee of puffed rice and mixture."

The man stood and searched in his pocket. Then he said, "Come this side." The man paid two and a half rupees to buy one samosa and a piece of Sandesh (sweets) and handed over it in a small paper parcel to the daughter.

The girl ate the sweets first. Then, suddenly she asked her father, "Papa! You must be hungry." Before the father could speak anything, she divided the samosa into two pieces and handed over half to her father. She ate the smaller half.

"It is good, Papa."

The man was holding an old tin drunk. The girl had a small bag. The cloth of the girl was in the trunk and the man's cloth was in the bag. The box was not heavy. The girl had only a pair of frocks, two old sarees of her mother, and a cherished doll. The rubber doll was purchased from the market in Bhawanipatna four years ago. The doll was not really bought for the daughter. It was meant for her baby brother, but the baby did not survive for long. He died before he was even one year old. It was not understood whether the girl was happy or sad after getting ownership of the doll of her dead brother. Her feeling was equally incomprehensible when her mother died of injuries sustained by bear attack.

"Rebati, it is good that she died. She was suffering. Now she will live happily with the stars in the heaven."

In the dark night looking at the cluster of stars, whether Rebati cried or laughed nobody knew.

"Hey! Be careful while walking on the road. You just escaped being trampled by a car," the man shouted while pulling the daughter from the middle of the road. Amid the noise of the road, the girl could not hear what her father said.

"We have to go a long way. We cannot walk the distance. Let us wait for a bus or a train."

The man had come to the city only once before this. With that half-known knowledge of the city, in half-Hindi half-Odia he tried to find the bus to take them to Satinath lane. It took him fifty minutes. There were lakhs of people, hundreds of streets in this city. Among those, many people could not tell where Satinath lane was. Half of them were not prepared to listen to his questions.

The man had first met Makhanlal Chaudhary of Satinath lane in Kesinga railway station. Amidst the smoke of cigarette, in mixed Hindi-Bangla Makhanlal said, "See, Banabasi! You will not face any trouble in reaching the address. If you go by a taxi, it will cost one hundred and ten rupees, but by bus you have to pay only eight rupees. I'm giving you one hundred and ten rupees. You go by whatever you choose. Remember 78-B, Satinath lane."

Mustering much courage, Banabasi had come to

this far with his daughter – from Kesinga to Calcutta. He decided to go to Satinath lane by paying eight rupees of bus fare. Only he had to recognize the bus number in the heavy rush. They got into a bus first; there was no place to sit. They had to stand all the way. They alighted from the bus and boarded another bus. The crowd had thinned. Rebati got a window seat. She was looking at the vastness of the city – people, motorcars, lights, buildings and the window. Among all these, the people were looking weakest and helpless.

During the bus journey, Banabasi was trying to talk to the co-passengers to reassure himself, but he did not know how to correctly use the language. Besides, the co-passengers were not in a mood to talk after a tiring day. When he had visited Calcutta earlier, he was not alone. There were four other persons from Kalahandi and Kandhamal with him. They had come with the hope that anyone with muscle can get a job in Calcutta – in cotton mill or in the harbor. But they returned hopeless because one could not get a job without recommendation. They visited and saw the magic house, the river Ganga, the crowded market and came back to their own land.

Rebati's mother insisted, "Go again. Try again. There are eight mouths to be fed at home. You cannot give up."

Now the family was reduced to six – the old parents, two useless sons, Rebati, and himself. The eldest son was twenty and the younger was fifteen. Both were good for nothing. They spent the day gossiping or getting into trouble. The daughter was calm and docile. She had wanted to study, but there was no teacher in the village school. The teacher had gone on leave before two years and had not returned yet. The school had been locked since then.

It was sad that Rebati's mother had suffered from the bear bite injury for four months and had died. The father had had to spend nearly one thousand rupees for the treatment. That was another sorrow. He had to sell his land to arrange the money, though Rebati's mother had strongly disagreed to sell the land. Lying on the mat smeared with pus and blood, Rebati's mother had said, "Don't sell the land. Do you think I will really survive? Why are you sacrificing the money?" A portion of the money from the sale of the land was sacrificed for her last rites.

After her death, the news spread in the locality that a big factory would be constructed in Kesinga. The government had finally listened to the poor after so long. The government would give employment to one thousand people.

Everyone was asking, "Which factory will be opened?"

"*Finning* mill," someone said (*as the illiterate villager could not pronounce spinning mill*). Spinning mill would be established in Kesinga.

"What is *finning*, brother? What is produced in that mill?"

It was found out that cotton would be used to produce thread. The baboos in Bhubaneswar called it spinning mill. The construction work of the factory started. The land demarcation work was done. Iron, cement and sand were procured. The baboos arrived, the contractor came. The work continued day and night.

People said, "Banabasi, the government is taking your land to build factory."

"My land?"

"Yes. There will be need of houses for the baboos and laborers of the factory. There was no land for that. Don't worry. Government will give you a job in the factory. Afterall, the government has taken your land."

"What job shall I get in a spinning mill, baboo?"

People did not know how to answer that question. Banabasi looked at his hands and legs. He was satisfied. He was capable of doing any kind of work. But the spinning mill was not completed. After constructing big buildings for the factory and houses for the baboos, the government found that its pocket was empty. There was no money left to buy machineries.

"Then what will happen?"

"What will happen? These houses, buildings will be sold."

While attempting to light a cigarette borrowed from the listener, a man remarked, "Why are you worried? The person who will buy this factory will give you a job. Your job is guaranteed."

Suddenly, a commotion erupted in the bus, snapping Banabasi back from his flashback. The bus stopped and people started talking loudly in Bengali, "The man will not survive… He has died." Banabasi enquired, "Dada! What happened?" Nobody replied to him. It was understood amidst the noise that a man had died under the wheel of the bus. But it was not possible to know whether the man was a traveler or a beggar or a poor man or an unemployed. Nevertheless, nobody had the will or eagerness to know it. All the passengers got down the bus in a hurry and got into other buses to reach their destination. Banabasi was the last to get down the bus. The daughter was terrified. So, he did not go near the dead man. To his good fortune, he got another bus immediately. Rebati occupied a seat and whispered, "Papa! I am scared."

"Why are you afraid. Perhaps, the man was a drunkard."

"No Papa. I am not talking about that man. I am afraid. Can I do it. if I can't…"

Makhanlal had said, "There is no problem, if she doesn't know dance. We will teach her. Then she will dance in the drama hall of Calcutta. She will act. She will get 100 rupees per month in addition to food during the training. After that she will get 1500 rupees per month."

Banabasi's eyes had widened in disbelief, astonishment and excitement: "So much of money!" The disbelief dispelled as, to his utter surprise, Banabasi's eager hands got 800 rupees. Makhanlal said, "Take this much for now. If your daughter dances well, you will get advance money every three months. If she gets some medal or prize, that will be yours."

"Among the government's numerous schemes, this is one," Makhanlal elaborated, "the government now recognizes that without the progress of women, this country cannot develop. Everything will come to a halt. To enhance the status of women, many dance schools have been established in Calcutta. Village girls must be trained to become good citizens of the nation. The honor of the country must be preserved."

Rebati was interested in dancing and singing from early childhood. After witnessing village dramas, she would mimic the performances at home, portraying characters like Yashoda, Radha, and the demon-slaying Goddess Durga. Upon learning that she would be going to Calcutta to study dance, her mind buzzed with excitement, conjuring vivid dreams of happiness. As she traveled by train to Calcutta, the rhythmic beat of her heart synced with the train's motion. Lost in anticipation of a new world, she happily savored pickle during the journey.

The crowd in the bus became less. It was a dark outside. Rebati whispered, "Papa!"

"What?"

Rebati did not say anything.

"Are you feeling hungry again?"

"No, Papa."

"What then?"

After a moment of silence, the girl uttered, "Papa, we will return."

"Return? Why?"

"I'm afraid."

The man did not know how to pacify her – by scolding or consoling. He was also a bit afraid – afraid of the unknown, the uncertain. Banabasi had agreed to Makhanlal's words as he had no other way. He was apprehensive, but he surrendered to hunger, poverty and helpless days.

Satinath lane... Satinath lane.

The bus conductor announced as if in a delirium. Banabasi came to sense. He pulled his daughter's hand and hurried out of the bus. Banabasi proceeded holding his daughter's hands as if he was pulling her unwillingly. His apprehension and anxiety were visible on the face like daylight. Someone from inside him was asking, "Didn't you really know? You knew it. You guessed everything right. Why are you hesitant now?"

Satinath lane was narrow and dark. Still there was no problem in finding house number 78-B. On the veranda was sitting a lungi clad half naked fat man. He could see the shadow of a man in darkness and asked in Bengali, "Who are you? What do you need?" Then he could recognize the visitor. He remembered the name also, "Who? Banabasi? So, finally you have come."

Makhanlal glanced at the shadow of Rebati in the darkness, "Oh! You have brought your daughter also. Come upstairs." Then he called someone from the house, "Sambhu *bhaya* (brother)! Come here. A new artist has come."

Makhanlal stood up and tightened his dhoti as if he was getting ready for wrestling. His muscular body shone by the street light.

"Banabasi, why are you standing? Sit here." Banabasi could not understand where to sit – the broken bench on the veranda or the oily mat or the stairs. He kept standing.

A man with dark moustache holding a long torch while smoking came out of the house. He said in Hindi, "What happened Makhanlal?"

"Sambhu *bhaya*, the artist I was talking about… the new artist from Kalahandi has come."

Leaning against darkness, Sambhu *bhaya* looked at Rebati and said, "This girl…" He spoke disapprovingly as if he rejected or did not like Rebati. Banabasi suddenly felt a heavy burden lifted from his chest. He breathed out deeply. He remembered that he was feeling thirsty.

"She is a good artist – a fresh artist. I have collected information," Makhanlal said like a school boy uttering recitation.

"What is her age?"

"Sixteen years."

"Sixteen years?"

Sambhu *bhaya* lit the torch on Rebati's face. Her face was not properly seen as she had lowered her head. Then the searching light of a torch fell on her chest, then on her thigh and waist.

"No. She is not sixteen. She must be 12 or 13."

Makhanlal resisted in a weak voice, "No, fifteen or sixteen for sure. She has not been properly fed. That is why her body has not developed. She will look different in six months here."

"Six months... damn it. Who will wait for so long? You know the supply is less now."

Sambhu *bhaya* was not happy that advance money of one year had been paid for the girl. He did not like the thoughtless work of Makhanlal and taking his face away from him called the girl, "Hey girl! Come here." Without looking at her father or anyone else, the girl approached Shambhu *bhaya* as if she was hypnotized.

Sambhu said, "Open it. Open your frock."

Makhanlal said in a weak voice, "Sambhu *bhaya*! Her father is here."

Then only Shambhu noticed the man – the man leaning against the faded pillar near the staircase.

"He is Banabasi, the father of the artist."

Shambhu asked Makhanlal, "Have you paid him for his return journey?"

After getting the answer in the affirmative, Shambhu indifferently said, "Why is he still here? He can go." Then he looked at Rebati and said, "Open your dress. No, here it is dark. I cannot see. Come inside the house." Rebati went inside the house slowly. She looked once at her father. Now her eyes did not look like the eyes of a thirteen years old girl, there was no wish for a rubber doll, there was no desire for visiting the zoo or the craving for a piece of pickle. Now there was a woman in the glance. There was no need to calculate her age any longer. That woman had understood that in the dark house a voluptuous future is waiting to jump into her. Fear no longer gripped her; she stood unshaken. She forgave the whole world unhesitant, where everyone else existed, but she did not exist. In fact, she never existed.

❑

Note:
- In the Odia original of the story there is a pun on the word "Shraddha." Shraddha is the Hindu ritual of offering made to the deceased person; when the word is used with money, it means unnecessary expenditure. In the translation the word "sacrifice" has been used due to absence of a near equivalent in the target language.

The Allure of Ghasi Lane

Kamalakanta Das

Nestled amidst expansive fields, far removed from the hustle of the village and its markets, stood a modest government dwelling with two small rooms, a thatched roof, and open all around. A small kitchen and a small toilet stood at a distance. To the south of the house lay *ghasi* lane, and *ganda* lane could be seen in the west. The *ghasis* were of the sweeper caste, the Dalits, underprivileged, and poor. The *gandas* were harijans of the *paana* caste, with a very low position in society. Additionally, it was a hilly, Garjat region, once under the reign of kings and aristocrats. In this region, the general populace harbored disdain for these two castes; hence, their dwelling was in the suburb area. These quarters belonged to the vicinity nearby. There was no boundary. If robbers attacked and stole even during the daytime, nobody would know.

  This dwelling was referred to as quarters, although its size suggested a fraction even smaller than a quarter, perhaps closer to an eighth or sixteenth. The house stood in this open, lonely place. That's why it was often locked. Who would stay here with the children? There was a fear of robbery. Crossing the field led to a big pond nearby, with a forest of teak and other plants visible in the distance. Beyond that lay the boundary walls of the jail and *khadal* lane. The *khadal* caste was also considered untouchable and of low status.

At dawn, about thirty women from *ghasi* lane went to different lanes of the town with containers and sticks, clad in dirty torn clothes, to clean latrines and roads. Dark, dirty, naked children followed their mothers, crying and calling out all the way. Men also set out to sweep different areas of the town. Some went with axes to the forest to bring firewood. The pigs of *ghasi* lane, along with their piglets, rushed here and there in search of food.

In *ganda* lane, many wove cloth. The women and children of the lane engaged themselves in making thread and weaving since the morning. Women in groups from *khadal* lane went out to work as laborers – with songs on their lips, flowers in their hair, and short, colorful, torn sarees on their bodies. Like a narrow fringe, their daily income was limited and inadequate.

They were neglected, Dalits, harijans of the society, but they provided service to the society. Still, there was no one to take care of their stomachs. Everyone else considered themselves their masters. Others thought that they were robbers, drunkards, and characterless. They hated them. Nobody paid attention to the fact that they retained their goodness despite poverty.

Despite people's caution, Minaketan Mohapatra decided to stay in the quarters with his young wife and four little children. He had come from Cuttack on transfer. In the evening, the light of a lantern was seen in his front veranda.

The *ghasi* women were returning from the market. In surprise, they stopped in the shade of the mango tree, which was in front of the veranda. A woman named Dwimati was the senior among them. She approached the veranda and inquired, "Who are you, mother of daughter? Where are you from? How will you stay alone in this quarters?"

The mother of the daughter, meaning the wife of Mr. Mohapatra, came to the veranda and asked, "Where is your house?"

Dwimati paid her respect and said, "Mother, my house is in *ghasi* lane. We are *ghasis*, your neighbor."

Rebati, the mother of the daughter and wife of Mr. Mohapatra, smilingly replied, "Why? You all are here. We have become your neighbor now. We will stand by you in your good and bad times, and you will stand in ours. Will you not guard our children?"

The mother of Kala, an old woman wearing a torn saree came close to Dwimati and said, "Mother, nobody ever told us such good words. We are *ghasis*. Nobody lives in this house because it is near *ghasi* and *ganda* lane. It is always locked. Where are you from, mother? Have you come on government transfer?"

Rebati said, "Yes, mother. We have been transferred from Cuttack."

"Where is baboo?"

"He has gone to the market."

"How many children do you have?"

"Three daughters and a son."

Dwimati said, "We will come, mother. Will you not hate us? We will come, sit, and talk. Will you not be angry?"

"No, mother. Why should I hate? Are you not humans? You come. We will sit and talk. Your children will come and play with ours."

A *ghasi* woman named Parbati came forward and

said, "No, mother. If you mix with us, the baboos here will hate you."

"Will people here hate us? Let them. We will mix with you."

"What is your caste, mother?"

"We are brahmins."

Dwimati stepped back and said, "You are brahmins; that means you are God?"

"No, mother. We are also humans like you."

"It is late now. I will come tomorrow. We are poor. Will you visit our lane, mother?"

"Yes, surely I will visit."

All the women left together. On the way, they said to each other, "They are good people."

In *ganda* lane, ninety percent of the families lived by weaving. But due to some problems in the controlled market, they were apprehensive about the availability of thread. They complained, "How will we manage? We couldn't even procure a single bundle of thread." Minaketan baboo assured them, "You will surely get it." He announced hope while sitting on a cot under the lower thatched roof of Bhakuda in *ganda* lane: "Surely you will obtain thread. Come together and establish a cooperative society."

Hundreds of men and women crowded near the veranda of Bhakuda. They greeted Minaketan baboo and said, "We're all together, but they are not providing us thread. For seven consecutive days, we return empty-handed. The inspector baboo does not allow us to go near him. Who will listen to us?"

Then, with the effort of Minaketan baboo and the cooperation of all of *ganda* lane, a cooperative society was formed. Plenty of thread was brought, good weaving tools were bought, and the rhythmic hum of work echoed through the lane day and night. A room was rented in Badbazaar to open a shop. Everyone in *ganda* lane said, "Mohapatra baboo is not a man, but he's a god."

Narottam's mother Thunki came with a bundle of greens. She stood near Minaketan baboo's veranda and said, "Mother, I've brought this bundle of greens for you. Please, accept it. You're like a mother to me, and your daughters are my sisters."

Rebati emerged from the kitchen and observed Thunki placing the greens on the veranda. She warmly welcomed her and said, "Come to the veranda, mother. Why are you standing outside? Why did you bring the greens?"

"We're of *ganda* caste, mother. How can we go to your veranda?"

Rebati pointed at the front room and told her, "Look there; who is that girl?"

Thunki startled and responded, "Oh, mother, that is Surabali, the daughter of Bhakudi of our lane. What is she doing? Is she reading? She's sitting beside your daughter."

With a smile, Rebati explained, "Yes, she is reading. Baboo has promised her father to take her to school today and enroll her."

"But who will tend to her goats for grazing?"

Thunki sighed and settled in a corner of the veranda. At that moment, Dwimati's daughter Bisnupriya from *ghasi* lane approached and called out, "Mother, what are you doing?"

"I'm coming; you come this way."

Within a month, the residents of *ganda* and *ghasi* lanes came to realize that the newcomer had come with their well-being in mind and harbored no animosity towards them. He was a good man. One day, Gadadhar *ghasi* and Lalmani *ghasi* came with tools and said, "Baboo sir! We are constructing a fence for your house. It won't take much time."

Minaketan baboo chuckled, "Gadadhar, you are all my fences? Let it remain open."

"No, baboo. That's not what we mean. We are saying that with a fence, pigs won't be able to enter."

"Alright, as you wish."

A canopy was set up near the house, and the field was leveled with layers of mud and cow dung. In the evening, the young and the old men, along with the women, gathered at the place. They discussed many things. Minaketan and his wife sat among them; the children played around. Passers-by commented, "This man has come from Cuttack; he may be a *ganda* or a *ghasi*." Sometimes they were left perplexed when they saw people from *khadal* lane sitting amidst the crowd.

In the morning, around 9:00 or 10:00 am, the *gauda* (caste of people who tend cows) woman would call out, "Take some buttermilk." This buttermilk, made from watery curd, was their source of income. The elderly woman Raibari would call from the door, "Oh mother of Muni, take some flat beans." In her sale of flat beans, her affection for Rebati and the children was evident. She would often spend some time chatting with them and occasionally give away onions for free. Sometimes, she would even eat watered rice from Rebati's hands.

In the dead of night, Kala's voice pierced through from the backyard, "Mother, please, open the door quickly. My husband is drunk and has followed, threatening to kill me." Rebati rose and unlatched the door. Kala hurried inside and spread the fringe of her saree before settling in the front room. Her two children nestled beside her. Baisnaba *ghasi*'s shouts echoed outside the house. He had dark complexion, broad chest, and a pair of prominent moustaches. Having served two six-month terms in prison for theft, he now stood drunk, demanding money from his wife Kala to buy liquor. When she refused, he flew into a rage, wielding a stick and threatening her life.

Standing on the veranda, he thundered, "Mother, you have sheltered my wife; release her to me. I will end her life today."

Minaketan baboo was not at home; he was away on business. It was midnight. With no one nearby to aid them, Rebati faced the drunken and erratic Baisnaba alone. Despite his reputation as a robber and his intoxicated state, Rebati remained resolute. She addressed him calmly, "Who is there? Is it Baisnaba?"

"Yes, mother, it is me."

Rebati's voice remained steady as she admonished him, "You are drunk and you are chasing your wife to beat her. She has sought refuge here; I cannot abandon her. Leave now. She will return in the morning. I appeal you to quit drink."

In his intoxicated state, he relented, "Let her rest, mother. The fault is mine. I am drunk. I am leaving, mother. Forgive me. I have made a mistake by drinking liquor. I will not do so again."

After that night, Baisnaba did not come for a month. Shame and remorse weighed heavily upon him as Minaketan and Rebati came to know of his drinking problem and the once formidable Baisnaba found himself humbled before their understanding and compassion.

Meanwhile, the daughter of Dasia *ghasi* Tilottama suffered from fever. Rebati rushed to her with medicine and sat beside her, offering words of comfort. The wife of Dasia, in gratitude, bowed before Rebati, took the dust from her feet and put on Tilottama's head as blessing for recovery.

Disaster struck the *ghasi* lane as huts caught fire. With the men absent, women cried out in distress. Concerned neighbors rushed from the nearby market, shouting advice from a distance, "Fetch water; stop your cries. Where are your menfolk?" But nobody ventured near because it was *ghasi* lane. Minaketan baboo arrived and cinched his loincloth, preparing to dive into work. *Ghasi* women handed water pots to him. Inspired by his example, some other men came forward to help. Meanwhile, Kala's mother writhed on the ground, crying loudly, "My utensils, my brass bowl and plate." These possessions were the entirety of her wealth. Minaketan baboo rescued those items from the flames and said, "Take your utensils; do not cry; go and fetch water."

"Thank you, sir, I am going."

With the pot in her hand, the old woman rushed to the pond with renewed determination. A sahib stood at a distance near his Jeep, while other baboos crowded around, gossiping: "Who is this man? He's not from *ghasi* lane." And someone remarked, "Perhaps, he is the relative of a *ghasi*. His attire suggests he has come from Kolkata or Tata."

He was Minaketan, the friend of *ghasi* lane, the relative of *ganda* lane, the brother of *khadal* lane, and the confidant of the Dalits, marginalized, poor, and harijans. Despite being scorned and insulted among the elite, in the harijan lane, he was revered as a leader, a mother, and a father.

The elderly man of royal lineage, Lalu Sahib, kept himself informed about Minaketan's activities regularly. He strolled in that direction and, standing beneath the bare mango tree, called out, "Baboo sir, are you home?"

Minaketan baboo came out and held his stick cautiously: "Namaskar, sir. You are older to me. I would prefer, if you address me by my name."

Lalu Sahib replied, "But you are a brahmin. You deserve respect."

Minaketan responded, "Sir, I am a harijan."

Lalu Sahib folded his hands and said, "Yet my head bows in reverence for harijans like you. Please, sit. Let us share our sorrows and joys."

Minaketan baboo brought another mat. Both of them sat and chatted for about an hour. While taking leave, they warmly greeted each other.

Janardan Guru of brahmin lane was a brahmin from the South. He had built his house and had been staying in that village. He spent a significant part of his childhood in Nadia, Nabadwip, and Brindaban. He wore a necklace of *tulsi* and sacred thread. He sang well and performed *kirtan* with instruments. Sometimes he would visit Minaketan baboo's home with his *dhol* (drum). Minaketan baboo played the cymbal. His melodious voice combined with the beautiful rhythm of the *dhol* and cymbal. Around the house, the veranda and below it, the old and young, daughters and daughters-in-law of *ganda* and *ghasi* lanes had crowded. It ended around 12:00 or 1:00 at night. *Hari bol, Hari Hari bol.*

Sanitation work was going on in *ghasi* lane. Minaketan was leading; women, men, children, and the elderly, all followed him.

Medicine was being distributed in *ghasi* lane.

Today, in *ganda* lane, a *kirtan* was being organized. While singing in the *kirtan*, the people of the lane carried brooms and containers, sweeping the road and repairing the potholes along the way.

A meeting was organized in *khadal* lane. The evening

school had opened; the teacher had arrived. Both old and young would study for two hours every day. The government had supplied slates, chalks, pencils, notebooks, and lanterns. In the end, the teacher would receive five rupees for each literate student as remuneration. It was not charity or sympathy; illiterates were being taught to become literate.

Everyone had assembled in *chamar* lane that day. Among them, Minaketan baboo and a high official from the industry department were sitting. They said, "Be united; you will receive machinery from the government. You will be trained in modern technologies to make shoes. The government will oversee the sale of shoes made by you. Your income will increase, and your economic condition will improve."

Hari bol. The sound of ululation could be heard. The silent and impoverished *chamar* lane buzzed with hope for happiness. The higher-caste baboos were brimming with jealousy: "It is not far when these lower-caste people will surpass us."

Rohini, an eighty-year-old woman, earned her livelihood by selling paan (betel leaves with spices). She selected good-quality betel leaves and brought them for Rebati, whom she affectionately called her grand daughter-in-law. Minaketan baboo referred to her as grandmother. Sometimes, she sat with Rebati and shared stories of her life. She brought flowers and fruits for Minaketan baboo's children, displaying much affection. She held a deep love and fondness for this outsider family.

Previously, the upper-caste people harbored hatred toward the lower castes. They didn't invite them into their homes or sit near them. Over time, those sentiments had diminished. Now, daughters and daughters-in-law from the officer's colony visited their home. The long-standing taboo of hatred for harijans was gradually being replaced by a love for humanity. Slowly, people would forget past grievances. Minds were evolving with the changing times. Old norms would shift; a new dawn would rise, and all would be equal in its light. Humanity would unite as one – an embodiment of flesh and blood, sorrow and joy, vice and virtue, justice and injustice. People would rise to divinity, shedding hatred and enmity. Within every person, divinity resides; one only needs to nurture it. Among Buddha, Jesus, Krishna, Prophet Mohammad, Ram, Rahim, Chaitanya, Nanak, Sankaracharya, Ramanuj, Kabir, who had ever harbored hatred toward humans? The inner sanctum of a person is the temple of God. How much time would it take to cleanse it?

Many people held government jobs, but Minaketan's work transcended his official duties. His transfer order arrived. He exchanged responsibilities with another person and began packing his belongings. The news spread rapidly through *ghasi* lane, *ganda* lane, the baboos' colony, *chamar* lane, and *khadal* lane. Everyone was sad – as if bidding farewell had cast a dark cloud over the entire area. Those who met him asked with somber faces, "Baboo sir, have you truly been transferred? Will you truly leave us?"

Those asking these questions found themselves unable to continue their conversation as tears welled in their eyes. Their voices quivered with sadness. Heaviness weighed on their tones, their lips trembled, and their hearts cried out as if they were bidding farewell to an intimate friend. Their minds urged them to stand in his way, to grasp his hand and implore him to stay.

It was time to bid farewell. Old Lalu Sahib, with his stick, had arrived. A woman, accompanied by a few children, entered their entrance room with a bowl of *kakara pitha* (stuffed sweet fried snacks). She wiped her wet eyes with her fringe. People from *ghasi* lane, *ganda* lane, and *khadal* lane had assembled around the quarters; everyone was crying. The luggage was carried to the bus station. Minaketan, his wife, and children came to the veranda; they were crying too. They struggled to speak while taking their leave. Minaketan held Kala's hand, attempting to say something, but words failed to emerge. Putariani tightly grasped Rebati's hands. Ranka's mother embraced her. Dwimati and Kala were crying loudly as they embraced them. The thief Baisnaba and Bhakuda lay at Minaketan's feet and said, "Don't go, baboo. When you came, our eyes opened. If you go, we will be blind again."

The upper caste and the lower caste had become one; there was no discrimination; only a flood of love prevailed. The rich and the poor, Lalu Sahib of the royal family, and Bhakuda *ghasi* had united. Untouchability had been eradicated.

Minaketan wiped his tears and said, "I cannot leave you all. I cannot forsake the allure of *ghasi* lane, even to enter heaven. I no longer care for my job. Get back my belongings from the station."

The old grandmother, Rohini, started crying from a distance. Her toothless mouth parted in a smile. With tears in her eyes and a smile on her lips, she approached and touched Minaketan baboo's cheek. "Tell mother not to sell the bullock," she said. The old grandmother smiled and cried simultaneously; the grandson cried and laughed too. The blend of smiles and tears was too beautiful and poignant to witness.

❑

Glossary

Baboo: A term used to address Hindu gentlemen, equivalent to Mr.
Baria: A tribal pronunciation of the Indian boar, known as barah.
Bhulia: Members of the weaver caste from western Odisha, renowned for their tie-dye fabrics, especially the Sambalpuri style.
Bideshi: A term meaning "foreigner," commonly used by villagers and uneducated individuals to refer to outsiders.
Chaita Parab: A month-long festival celebrated by tribal communities during Chaitra. It involves wearing new clothes, animal sacrifices, feasting, drinking, singing, and dancing.
Chamar: A Dalit community belonging to the Scheduled Caste, traditionally associated with leatherwork.
Chara: An Indian forest fruit.
Dhangri: A term referring to a young woman.
Dhol: A double-sided Indian drum often played during celebrations and processions.
Dung-dunga: A traditional musical instrument.
Ganda: A Scheduled Caste weaver community originating from Western Odisha, distinct from the Gond community.
Gauda: An Indian caste from Odisha, traditionally

	involved in dairy farming and cattle herding.
Ghasi:	A Scheduled Caste community in Odisha, historically marginalized and subjected to social injustice, untouchability, and economic exploitation.
Handia:	Country liquor, a type of rice beer originating from the Indian subcontinent.
Hari bol:	A chant invoking the name of the Lord.
Juhar:	A traditional way of greeting.
Kakara pitha:	A sweet deep-fried cake from Odisha, often offered to temple deities and served hot or cold during festivals.
Kendu:	Indian forest persimmon, a fruit.
Khadal:	A Scheduled Caste community in Odisha.
Kirtana:	A form of musical narration or shared recitation, particularly associated with spiritual or religious themes, prevalent in Hindu religion.
Kondh:	The Kondhs, also spelled Kondha and Kandha, are an indigenous Adivasi/tribal community in India. Traditionally hunter-gatherers, they are categorized into hill-dwelling Kondhs and plain-dwelling Kondhs for census purposes, although they primarily identify themselves by specific clans (e.g., dangaria kondh and kutia kondh as seen in "Daughter of Niyamagiri"). While owning large tracts of fertile land, Kondhs maintain their connection to the forests by practicing hunting, gathering, and slash-and-burn agriculture. They speak the Kui language.

	Kandhamal district in Odisha, named after the tribe, has a fifty-five percent Kondh population.
Koupin:	A loincloth worn by men in the Indian subcontinent as undergarments.
Kusuma:	Ceylon Oak, also known as lac tree or gum lac tree.
Mahula:	Butternut, a type of fruit.
Mahuri:	A traditional wind instrument originating from Odisha, often played during auspicious occasions like weddings. The person who plays the mahuri is known as a Mahuria.
Paan:	Betel leaf combined with spices.
Paana:	A Dalit community in Odisha, officially recognized as Scheduled Caste in Bihar, West Bengal, and Jharkhand.
Padri:	A term referring to a Christian priest or father.
Sahukar:	A moneylender.
Shabar:	A tribe primarily residing in Odisha and West Bengal.
Tulsi:	Holy basil, revered by Hindus for its spiritual significance. A Tulsi necklace, crafted from holy basil wood, symbolizes devotion, purity, and spiritual growth.

Bio-notes of the Authors:

Abani Kumar Baral:
Abani Kumar Baral (1935-2013) was an eminent educationist, columnist, author and socialist leader from Odisha. He has authored more than twenty books including biographies, travelogues and novels. His Odia novels *Premar Aneswanare Gotia Taruni* (*A Woman in Search of Love*), and *Aparahnara Chhai* (*Shadow of the Evening*) are highly acclaimed creations.

Bhagabati Charan Panigrahi:
Bhagabati Charan Panigrahi (1908-1943) was a notable Odia writer and a revolutionary figure in India's freedom struggle. As a founding member of Netaji's Forward Bloc and the founding secretary of the Communist Party of India in Odisha, he played a pivotal role in shaping the political landscape. Despite his short literary career, Panigrahi authored around a dozen short stories, including the renowned "Shikaar," which depicted the plight of Odisha's tribal communities under British oppression. This story was later adapted into the film "Mrigayaa" by Mrinal Sen in 1976, and in 2016, an Odia language play based on the same narrative was staged. In November 1935, Panigrahi, along with Ananta Patnaik and others,

established the literary organization "Nabayuga Sahitya Sansad," which quickly gained prominence for fostering new ideas in modern Odia literature. Additionally, in 1936, he edited the magazine *Adhunika*, further contributing to the literary discourse of his time. Panigrahi's life and work remain influential, reflecting his commitment to both literature and revolution.

Bhubaneswar Behera:
Bhubaneswar Behera (1916-2001) was an engineer, writer and scholar from the Kalahandi district of Odisha. Prior to joining the engineering faculty, Behera initiated a monthly Odia magazine named *Saptarshi* with the aim of fostering a culture of reading and writing in Odia among students. He personally contributed editorials to the magazine, swiftly establishing himself as a beloved Odia prose writer. His travelogue in Odia titled *Paschima Africa re Odia Dhenki* has been adopted as a textbook in many universities across his home state. Behera authored eight books in Odia, with his collection of essays, *Suna Parikshya*, earning him the prestigious Odisha Sahitya Academy Award. Additionally, his autobiographical narrative, *Gaon-ra-Dhaka*, was honored with the prestigious Sarala Award.

Durga Madhav Mishra:
Durga Madhab Mishra (1929-1997), a noted Odia literary figure, was an Indian Police Service officer and the first Odia to serve as Director General of the Central Industrial Security Force (CISF). He was an editor, poet, novelist and translator at the same time. He won the Odisha Sahitya Akademi Award (1982) for

his short story collection *Nishada ra Nishabda Barana* (*The Silent Exclusion of the Night*).

Gayatri Saraf:
Gayatri Saraf (born 17 August 1952) is an Indian feminist writer. Recognized for her teaching prowess, she received the President's Award in 2004. Her popular works of fiction include *Itabhati ra Shilpi, Kathayana-1, Panata Kanire Ghara, Asidha Adhyaya, Kathayana-2, Kehi Ta Jane,* and *Srestha Galpa.* In 2017, she was honored with the Central Sahitya Academy Award for her collection *Itabhati ra Shilpi.* She served as the Vice-President of Odisha Sahitya Academy from 2015 to 2018.

Kamalakanta Das:
Kamalakanta Das, born in 1906, dedicated his life to literature, finding acclaim as a novelist primarily through his debut work *Bou* (*Mother*). Despite facing physical challenges later on, he continued his prolific writing career, producing twenty-four novels, six short story collections, and various essays and poems. In 1935, *Ashrita* was published, followed by *Saradi Nani, Manara Dau, Chabis Number Cabin, Manisa ra Dabi, Nartaki, Sadar Mafsal,* and many others in subsequent years. His narratives skillfully depicted both urban and rural life, particularly focusing on pre-independence village settings, while fearlessly addressing social issues like untouchability and corruption. Alongside his literary pursuits, Das also excelled as a painter and artist. His contributions were recognized with honors from the Orissa Sahitya Akademi and Kalavinod, solidifying his enduring legacy in Odia literature.

Pranabandhu Kar:

Pranabandhu Kar (1914-1988), a playwright and short story writer, is regarded as a pioneer of modern Odia literature. As a professional educator, he drew on everyday events and situations to create stories that captivate both the readers and the authors. He struggled with poverty, sluggishness, frustrations, and disappointments, yet overall he was an optimist and enjoyed life. As a result, his writings often exude positivism, highlighting the good in his characters through fine psychoanalysis. Pranabandhu Kar wrote thirty-five plays and more than fifty short stories. The short stories were featured in various magazines and later a compilation of these stories was published as *Pranabandhu Kar: Galpa Samagra*, by Vidyapuri publishers in 2014. He set trends in Odia plays and short stories with his style, technique, and eagerness to try new things. His works have garnered him accolades and honours from the Central Sahitya Akademi, Central Dance-Drama Akademi, Odisha Sahitya Akademi, and many other esteemed organisations.

Rajat Mohapatra:

Rajat Mohapatra (1950-2012), born in Dhenkanal in the state of Odisha, India, worked as a lecturer of English in different Government colleges and retired as a Deputy Director from Directorate of Higher Education, Odisha. He earned accolades as a writer as well as a translator of short stories. His well-known publications include the Odia short story collections *Apaharana* (*Kidnapped*), 2002 and *Shunya Santarana* (*Swimming in the Void*), 2014.

Tarunakanti Mishra:
Tarun Kanti Mishra was born on 2nd August, 1950 in the hill-town of Keonjhar, in the state of Odisha, India. An Indian Administrative Service officer of 1975 batch, he served in different capacities till 2010. As regard to his literary career, his first anthology of short stories appeared in 1968, when he was an undergraduate student of B.J.B. College, Bhubaneswar. He has also authored a novel against the backdrop of Dandakaranya, a vast territory inhabited by immigrants of erstwhile East Pakistan and a large tribal population. So far Shri Mishra has published 18 anthologies of short stories and a novel. "Komal Gandhar," "Kagajara Phula," "Abarta," and "Bisalya" are some of his popular stories.

Black Eagle Books

www.blackeaglebooks.org
info@blackeaglebooks.org

Black Eagle Books, an independent publisher, was founded as a nonprofit organization in April, 2019. It is our mission to connect and engage the Indian diaspora and the world at large with the best of works of world literature published on a collaborative platform, with special emphasis on foregrounding Contemporary Classics and New Writing.

www.ingramcontent.com/pod-product-compliance
Lightning Source LLC
Chambersburg PA
CBHW060617080526
44585CB00013B/869